The Complete
Barrack-Room Ballads

THE COMPLETE

BARRACK-ROOM BALLADS

OF RUDYARD KIPLING

EDITED BY

CHARLES CARRINGTON

LONDON

METHUEN & CO LTD

1973

821
KIP

First published 1973 by Methuen & Co Ltd
11 New Fetter Lane, London EC4
© *1973 Charles Carrington*
Printed in Great Britain by
Butler & Tanner Ltd
Frome and London

SBN (hardbound) 416 78140 3
SBN (Paperback) 416 78150 0

Preface and
Acknowledgements

Kipling's *Barrack-Room Ballads*, a distinct section of his work and a new genre in English literature, have not been collected hitherto in a single volume, though for many years they were the most familiar and widely quoted of all contemporary verses throughout the English-speaking world. The first dozen of them appeared in periodicals in England and America during 1890, and were brought together in the volume called *Barrack-Room Ballads and Other Verses* (1892). A second series appeared in *The Seven Seas* (1896) and a third series, dealing with the Boer War, in *The Five Nations* (1903). It was these volumes that maintained the popularity of the ballads over so many years. During the First World War Kipling composed an anthology of soldiers' epitaphs included in *The Years Between* (1919) which form a fitting conclusion to this portrait-gallery of an army. In these four volumes he did not arrange the ballads in a logical order but in the order of publication. I have thought it helpful to the reader to rearrange them by subjects. In each series I have followed the progress of a soldier's life: what he hears as a young recruit; the voyage to the East; barrack life; campaigning; and the return to England.

When deciding what is and what is not a barrack-room ballad, I had less difficulty than I expected, and found it necessary to include

v

only four short pieces from Kipling's 20,000 lines of published verse other than the four groups mentioned above. The problems that have occupied me are linguistic and historical: most of the ballads are written in the London vernacular to which little attention has been given by students. In this field I have been much stimulated by Peter Keating's book, *The Working-Classes in Victorian Fiction*, and helped by the advice of Eric Partridge; the historical problem is that the soldiers' slang has become unintelligible to a generation that does not much remember the old regular army, still less the British-Indian army.

On service customs and traditions I have received much help from Major-General B. P. Hughes, Colonel L. H. Landon, Commander C. H. Drage RN and Mr Philip Mason. I also wish to thank my colleagues of the Kipling Society, Colonel A. E. Bagwell-Purefoy, Mr R. Lancelyn Green and Mr R. E. Harbord, for frequent advice; Mrs J. Small for secretarial help, and my wife, always my kindest and most exacting critic.

London, December 1972   C. E. C.

Contents

Preface and Acknowledgements   page v

Index of First Lines   xi

Introduction

The biographical background   *1*

The ballads   *9*

The text   *13*

Kipling's use of dialect   *14*

Kipling and the army   *19*

I Barrack-Room Ballads
(from *Barrack-Room Ballads and other Verses*, 1892)

1 The Widow at Windsor   *30*
2 Tommy   *31*
3 The Young British Soldier   *33*
4 Belts   *36*
5 Cells   *37*
6 Route Marchin'   *39*
7 Screw-Guns   *40*

vii

8 Oonts *43*

9 The Widow's Party *44*

10 Gentlemen-Rankers *46*

11 'Snarleyow' *48*

12 Ford o' Kabul River *49*

13 Gunga Din *51*

14 'Fuzzy-Wuzzy' *54*

15 Loot *56*

16 Danny Deever *59*

17 Troopin' *61*

18 Soldier, Soldier *62*

19 Mandalay *64*

20 Shillin' a Day *67*

II Barrack-Room Ballads

(all but Nos. 31 and 36 from *The Seven Seas,* 1896)

21 'Back to the Army Again' *70*

22 'Birds of Prey' March *72*

23 The 'Eathen *74*

24 'The Men that fought at Minden' *77*

25 Bill 'Awkins *79*

26 The Shut-Eye Sentry *80*

27 The Sergeant's Weddin' *82*

28 The Mother-Lodge *84*

29 Sappers *87*

30 'Soldier an' Sailor Too' *89*

31 'Bobs' *92*

32 The Jacket *94*

33 That Day *96*

34 Cholera Camp *98*

35 'Follow Me 'Ome' *100*

36 'My girl she give me the go onst' *101*

37 The Ladies *103*

38 'Mary, pity Women!' *105*

39 For To Admire *107*

Contents

III Service Songs
(all but No. 40 from *The Five Nations*, 1903)

40 The Absent-Minded Beggar *111*
41 Stellenbosh *113*
42 Two Kopjes *115*
43 The Instructor *117*
44 Boots *118*
45 The Married Man *120*
46 Ubique *122*
47 Columns *123*
48 M. I. *126*
49 Lichtenberg *129*
50 The Parting of the Columns *131*
51 Half-Ballad of Waterval *133*
52 Bridge-Guard in the Karroo *134*
53 'Wilful-Missing' *137*
54 Piet *138*
55 Chant-Pagan *140*
56 The Return *143*
57 The Settler *145*

IV Epitaphs of the Great War
(from *The Years Between*, 1919)

Only epitaphs of British soldiers are reprinted here.

58 'Equality of Sacrifice' *149*
59 A Servant *149*
60 A Son *149*
61 An Only Son *150*
62 Ex-Clerk *150*
63 The Wonder *150*
64 Hindu Sepoy in France *150*
65 The Beginner *151*

66 The Favour *151*
67 The Refined Man *151*
68 The Coward *151*
69 The Sleepy Sentinel *152*
70 Shock *152*
71 Salonikan Grave *152*
72 Native Water-Carrier (M.E.F.) *152*
73 Bombed in London *153*
74 Batteries out of Ammunition *153*
75 Common Form *153*
76 Gethsemane *153*

Explanatory Notes *155*

Index of First Lines

'As anybody seen Bill 'Awkins *79*

As I was spittin' into the Ditch *89*

At times when under cover I 'ave said *117*

'Ave you 'eard o' the Widow at Windsor *30*

By the old Moulmein Pagoda *64*

Epitaphs of the Great War (not listed separately) *149*

'E was warned agin 'er *82*

Here where my fresh-turned furrows run *145*

I do not love my Empire's foes *138*

If you've ever stole a pheasant-egg *56*

I'm 'ere in a ticky ulster *70*

It got beyond all orders *96*

I've a head like a concertina *37*

I've taken my fun where I've found it *103*

I went into a public-'ouse *31*

I wish my mother could see me now *126*

Kabul town's by Kabul river *49*

March! The mud is cakin' good *72*

Me that 'ave been what I've been *140*

My girl, she give me the go onst *101*

My name is O'Kelly *67*

Only two African Kopjes *115*
Out o' the wilderness, dusty an' dry *123*
Peace is declared an' I return *143*
Sez the Junior Orderly Sergeant *80*
Smells are surer than sounds or sights *129*
Smokin' my pipe on the mountings *40*
'Soldier, soldier come from the wars *62*
Sudden, the desert changes *134*
The bachelor 'e fights for one *120*
The 'eathen in 'is blindness *74*
The Garden called Gethsemane *153*
The General 'eard the firin' on the flank *113*
The Injian Ocean sets an' smiles *107*
The men that fought at Minden *77*
There is a word you often see *122*
There is a world outside the one you know *137*
There's a little red-faced man *92*
There was a row in Silver Street *36*
There was no one like 'im, 'Orse or Foot *100*
There was Rundle, Station Master *84*
This 'appened in a battle to a battery *48*
Through the Plagues of Egyp' *94*
To the legion of the lost ones *46*
Troopin', troopin', troopin' *61*
We're foot-slog—slog—slog—sloggin' *118*
We're marchin' on relief over Injia's sunny plains *40*
We've fought with many men acrost the seas *54*
We've got the cholerer in camp *98*
We've rode and fought and ate and drunk *131*
'What are the bugles blowin' for *59*
When by the labour of my 'ands *133*
When the 'arf-made recruity goes out *33*
When the Waters were dried an' the Earth did appear *87*
When you've shouted 'Rule Britannia' *111*
'Where have you been this while away *44*

Index of First Lines

Wot makes the soldier's 'eart to penk   *43*
You call yourself a man   *105*
You may talk o' gin and beer   *51*

Introduction

When Rudyard Kipling, aged not quite twenty-four, came to London in October 1889 to seek his fortune, he soon discovered that for him the streets were indeed paved with gold. Not often in literary history has there been so sudden and continuing a success story. 'Each new boom is more portentous than the last' said his wise old father a few months later, as Rudyard unloaded on a greedy public a succession of reprints in verse and prose, written during his apprenticeship with an Indian newspaper. They were followed by a whole volume of new short stories based upon his Indian experience, a novel, *The Light that Failed*, which was not altogether successful in that mode but which has never since then been out of print; and, at the same time, month by month, a series of verses about British soldiers, which he then called 'barrack-room ballads'. The thirteen original soldier pieces first appeared between February and July 1890, in the *Scots Observer*, a literary weekly edited by W. E. Henley, a great patron of young writers. It is interesting to notice that these numbers of this journal also contained early verses by W. B. Yeats. Kipling's ballads attracted an immediate attention from the critics that was only the beginning of their fame. They escaped from the literary salons and spread like a bushfire into the wide world, into the public houses and 'the

I

The Complete Barrack-Room Ballads

Halls'; they were set to music and sung at 'smoking concerts'; were recited, quoted, copied, anthologized, translated; and they reached their widest circulation in 1892 when he collected them, with some miscellaneous pieces, in the volume entitled *Barrack-Room Ballads, and Other Verses* which for thirty or forty years was the most popular book of verse in the English-speaking world, as popular in America as in England. It has been reprinted in authorized editions more than seventy times, enormously 'pirated' in unauthorized editions. These soldier ballads supply four columns of entries to the *Oxford Book of Quotations*.

At the first onset of publicity, when Kipling's name seemed to be always in the news, the critics' most consistent reaction was astonishment. This young man was an original, quite out of key with the tendencies of the *coteries* whose work was to be exemplified, a few years later, in *The Yellow Book*. Yet he could not be ignored even by the most refined of his contemporaries. He was firmly placed as a star in the literary galaxy by a leader writer for *The Times* (25 March 1890) – now known to be Mr Humphry Ward – who compared Kipling with Maupassant and hailed him as 'the discoverer of "Tommy Atkins" as a hero of realistic romance'. Oscar Wilde in a well-known essay said he makes one feel 'as if one were seated under a palm tree reading life by superb flashes of vulgarity'. Henry James described him in a private letter as 'the most complete man of genius (as distinct from fine intelligence) that I have ever known'. In a review he wrote that Kipling 'never arranges or glosses or falsifies, but goes straight for the common and the characteristic'. Shades of doubt soon began to cloud James's enthusiasm though he was, and remained, Kipling's close friend. In another private letter he wrote of the *Barrack-Room Ballads* and what followed them in these terms: 'he has come down steadily from the simple in subject to the more simple – from the Anglo-Indians to the natives, from the natives to the Tommies, from the Tommies to the quadrupeds, from the quadrupeds to the fish, and from the fish to the engines and screws', a mild joke that reflects more painfully upon James's sense of values than upon Kipling's

Introduction

literary progress. No doubt something was amiss, and it was noticed very early in his career by a writer in the *Scots Observer* itself (10 May 1890), perhaps W. E. Henley, perhaps Professor D. Masson, the learned editor of Milton. For in spite of his admitted genius, there was a vulgar streak in Kipling that it was difficult to account for.

In writing English, he [Kipling] is often inadequate, he is often pert, and he is sometimes even common; but in dialect he is almost always an artist. . . . The material is of the vilest, the very dregs of language . . . but the artist has produced an effect by the orchestration, as it were, of such low-lived and degraded vocables as (say) the equivalents of 'bloomin'' and 'beggar', that in its way is comparable to those great Miltonic polysyllables which seem to have been dictated by Apollo himself.

Here is praise and blame indeed, and astonishment: but I shall return later to Kipling's use of dialect.

There was a certain admixture of jealousy in the work of some reviewers who resented the instantaneous success of this brash outsider, this young man from nowhere, who ignored the modish cult of Art for Art's Sake, and paid no attention whatever to the strictures of his seniors. He followed his own Cockney muse and made money. The spate of productivity did his reputation little good. He was 'the comet of a season', reviewers said; 'he had gone up like a rocket and would come down like the stick'. Much of the hostility that built up against him was a reaction to the uncritical publicity that he attracted, and in later years he was still condemned for juvenile faults in his early work, written and rushed into print too rapidly, faults which are not to be found in the verse and prose of his maturity.

Kipling's life can be easily divided into phases and periods. Born at Bombay in 1865, he enjoyed a happy infancy that gave him a deep love for India and the Indians. His father, an artist and ethnologist, was an authority on Indian arts and crafts; his mother, one of the celebrated Macdonald sisters, belonged to the pre-Raphaelite circle and was on terms of friendship with the Morrises and the Rossettis as well as with her brother-in-law, Burne-Jones. Young Rudyard was far from being the ignorant 'colonial' he was supposed to be. Like other Anglo-Indian children in those days when there was no protection against tropical disease, he had been sent 'home' to be brought up by foster parents in a strict evangelical family at Southsea, where he was unhappy, as well he might be, though the tale of his ill-treatment has perhaps been exaggerated. At sixteen he returned to a cordial home life with his parents in India.

For six years he lived in what is now Pakistan, at Lahore, one of the most picturesque cities of Islam. It had passed under the rule of the Sikhs, a martial Hindu sect, after the collapse of the Mogul empire; and from the Sikhs it had passed to the British only forty years before young Kipling's arrival. Old men could well remember the Sikh monarchy of Runjit Singh, but at heart Lahore was still, as it is today, a Moslem capital. At scarcely seventeen years old, Kipling became assistant editor of the *Civil and Military Gazette*. After sending his newspaper to press he would pass long hours of the night wandering alone in the old walled city, observing that seamy side of life that is exposed to a press reporter. Yet he was not the raffish adventurer he was afterwards supposed to have been, but essentially domestic in habit, living at home, in Anglo-Indian style, with his parents and his charming young sister to whom he was devoted. In the cool season Lahore has a bracing climate but, when the feverish hot weather came to an India with, as yet, no refrigeration, no airconditioning, he was left alone in the blistering heat while his parents went off to a hill station, and was lucky if he could join them for a three-week holiday at Simla, the summer capital of British India. In his last year he was sent 700 miles down-country to work on a more important newspaper at Allahabad which, in spite of its name, is a Hindu city on the sacred river Ganges. Here he saw Hindustan, and from here his editor dispatched him as a special correspondent all over northern India. This experience, backed by his father's encyclopedic knowledge,

4

Introduction

made him free of a society that the 'heaven-born' governing class did not always appreciate.

Before his twentieth year he had begun to print light verse and short stories that attracted attention, with an ever widening outlook, anticipating Henry James's sneer in one of his most quoted (and most often misquoted) ballads, which was written just before he left India, in 1889.

> There is neither East nor West, Border, nor Breed, nor Birth,
> When two strong men stand face to face, though they come from
>   the ends of the earth.

He wrote not only of the vice-regal court and its gossip, but of engineers and district officers, law courts and opium dens, cholera epidemics and race riots, illicit love affairs across caste rules, dropouts from British society. With loving sympathy he visualized the Indian scene, writing delightfully of Indian children; and, rather late in the day, he came to the British 'Tommies', a new low caste in caste-ridden India, recruited from the lowest of unskilled labourers, scarcely to be ranked as *sahibs*. What sort of men were they, then, this fellowship of professional fighters, who rejected the proprieties and inhibitions of Victorian society, who appeared sometimes in the police court news as drunken disorderly reprobates, and sometimes as heroes of romance, the 'Thin Red Line' of Balaclava, the storming column of Delhi, the defenders of Rorke's Drift. Search English literature and you will find no adequate account of the British soldier, what he thought of his officers, and what he talked about the night before the battle, between Shakespeare's *Henry V* and Kipling's *Barrack-Room Ballads*. The British tradition was not favourable to soldiers; ever since Cromwell's day, hostility to a standing army had been an underlying factor in British politics. The sailor, the 'jolly Jack Tar', was the national hero, not the soldier.

But we have not come far with Kipling's story. After leaving India he made a long sea voyage at least once in every year, and the Kipling who was already well known as the writer on British

India and the British army acquired a new fame as a writer on ships, the sea and the romance of machinery. Early in 1892 he married an American wife with whom he settled for four years in Vermont. Some critics will claim that his American period produced his best work, or at least his best-selling work, the *Jungle Books*, *Captains Courageous*, the stories collected as *Many Inventions* and *The Day's Work* and the volume of verse called *The Seven Seas*. It can hardly be disputed that at this time, when he wrote with deliberation, scrutinizing every line before letting it go to press, the casual, defiant young Kipling had disappeared, to be replaced by a conscientious craftsman with a message to deliver, although perhaps his message was not to everyone's taste. *The Seven Seas* included a second series of 'barrack-room ballads' which still derived from his Indian experience, and were expressed in the same form as the first series, but gave a more thoughtful comment on the soldier's life.

This was a period of rapid social change in the Western countries; and in Asia, too, though Kipling may have been slow to notice it. *Kim* (1899), which many critics select as his masterpiece, was his valediction to India, and surely the best book about India by any European. He never revisited India. In 1896 the Kiplings returned to England though for several years ill-health obliged Rudyard to avoid the English winters, which they spent in South Africa. This, he said, was his 'political period' and the years 1897–1905 were for him, as for the Anglo-Saxon race in general, the age of imperialism. The British, to whom he addressed his warning, 'Recessional' (1897) and the Americans to whom he addressed his appeal, 'The White Man's Burden' (1899), were both engaged in overseas campaigns, the Anglo-Boer War and the Spanish-American War which were fought in a very different manner from the old rough combats on the frontiers, and with soldiers of quite another type. These wars were popular, in every sense of the word; the policy in both countries was supported by majorities in the elections of 1900; and in both countries scores of thousands volunteered to fight in distant battles which would bring them

Introduction

hardship and danger with no material reward. Had such a thing happened before? Kipling served as a war correspondent in South Africa and again produced a series of soldiers' ballads, but no longer of the barrack room, though they repeated the technique of the earlier series. He preferred to call them 'Service Songs'.

England had now known thirty years of public elementary education with the consequence that literacy, with a cheap and free press, gave the volunteers of 1899 a better understanding of the issues at stake. The questionings and doubts of the Boer War ballads (collected in *The Five Nations*, 1903) probe deeper than did the crude comments of the Tommies of the former generation, but a change in public taste prevented this book from winning such wide approval as his earlier verses.

After this prolonged war which had shaken the complacent sadly there was a reaction against the imperialism of the jubilee years. The Liberals came into power under a leader who had once been regarded by his opponents as a 'pro-Boer'. Not only imperialism but 'Kiplingism' went out of fashion with the *avant-garde*. The social reforms of the Edwardian age, which we tend to see as the foundations of the modern welfare state, aroused no enthusiasm in the breast of Kipling who did not relish the prospect of a Fabian utopia. Yet it was Kipling, almost alone, who had recognized the potent urges of the generation that extended Western technology over the whole surface of the globe; 'What should they know of England who only England know' he had written. In the literary world, Kipling, was 'out on a limb'. He never met H. G. Wells, and met Bernard Shaw only once, at Hardy's funeral.

In 1902 he had withdrawn to Burwash, a remote Sussex village, where he spent the last thirty years of his life as a literary recluse. Successful, rich, absorbed in his family circle, protected from intruders by his possessive wife, he lived as he chose, simply, selecting his own friends, writing at his own pace in verse and prose, often now on local themes, England and Sussex and their history. Still one of the world's best-selling authors, he never courted publicity, declined public honours, made no concessions to changing

7

taste, either in his message or in his style. The critics, always on the lookout for some new thing, passed Kipling by and forgot him, while his books, new and old, were bought, read and quoted everywhere. His juvenile stories, composed for his own children, became known to literate families throughout the world; and a new peak of influence with the general public emerged with the didactic verse called 'If' (1910), propounding the Emersonian doctrine of self-reliance, an inspiration to the whole generation that fought in the First World War. Aggressively, contemptuously, he derided the soft optimism of the Liberals in a world that to him suggested no rosy future. Stoic and pessimist, he clung to traditional standards of conduct. The prophetic Kipling made occasional oracular utterances that appeared on the middle page of *The Times* like voices from the past: his rare interventions in actual politics were imprudent.

His life was clouded by two domestic misfortunes: the deaths of a beloved daughter in 1899 and of his only son in the battle of Loos, 1915. Each of these losses deepened his compassion for the bleakness of human circumstances, though his impish, sometimes cruel sense of humour never failed. His later stories were increasingly involved and intricate, dealing no longer with incidents in the lives of young soldiers and sailors but with the mental processes of mature adults, especially of middle-aged women, stories that recall the subject-matter, but not the style, of Henry James. Kipling's compact control of words, his unshrinking regard for facts, however distasteful, his talent for visualizing a scene in a few phrases were more striking even than in his youth. As he grew older and his health deteriorated, the problem of pain obsessed him. The 'breaking-strain', the intolerable pressure of the twentieth century was his constant theme, especially in delayed symptoms of war neuroses. Even before his death the critics were beginning to reconsider their verdict. His range had been so wide and his public repute so long sustained, his name aroused such passionate like or dislike, that he could not be dismissed as a mere patriotic writer. He had never been the imperial boaster he was supposed to be.

Introduction

His hymn of empire, 'Recessional', was not a paean of pride but a call for humility. In the end, nothing counted for him but human values. A pessimist like Hardy, he faced a dark future, and long foretold the Second World War, which he did not live to see. Kipling died in January 1936, three days before King George V, who had been his friend.

It was not until 1941 that T. S. Eliot, then at the height of his reputation, restored Kipling to a place on Mount Parnassus, not without misgivings. Our greatest storyteller, no doubt, but was he a poet? Perhaps the ballads were not more than 'great verse', whatever that distinction was supposed to mean. W. B. Yeats, too, in his preface to the *Oxford Book of Modern Verse*, admitted to being puzzled by Kipling's art which he admired but could not classify. It was the Cockney ballads, especially 'Danny Deever,' that fascinated him as a unique phenomenon in English literature. When analysing them, we should recall that they constitute only a small part of Kipling's achievement, and belong to the first half of his life.

THE BALLADS

What are the features that distinguish Kipling's 'barrack-room ballads' from other army folklore? They are dramatic monologues, or occasionally dialogues, recited in character, and it is plain that in them fictitious persons are expressing their own sentiments and notions of army life, in a language that is appropriate. There are heroes and cowards among the speakers, honest men and rogues, thoughtless and thoughtful men, and even a few women of the camp, a gallery of self-portraits, and all different. The title of this book might be 'Tommy This or Tommy That', or it might be 'Single men in Barricks most Remarkable like You'. Most of the speakers use the vernacular of the London working class which Kipling was the first author to treat as a dialect with a right to be taken seriously, like Hardy's Wessex or Burns's lowland Scottish. He is skilful at conveying slight distinctions in manners of speech by emphasis, word order and rhythm; and the variation between speakers is remarkable. Technically Kipling's versification is accomplished. Every word seems to fall naturally into place, and there are no forced rhymes, no conventional epithets, no particles stuffed in to pad out a line; or had I better say that he reveals few of these faults in comparison with some poets of greater reputation? His internal rhymes are worth studying. Faults of composition, as well as of good taste, there are indeed, but they are errors of excess. He may overstate his case, hammer home a moral with which we have already agreed – or disagreed. The rare bad lines fail through too much compression of the material.

As Henry James said, Kipling never arranges, or glosses, or falsifies. If one of his characters speaks brutally or sentimentally, it is with the author's precise intention. It is absurd to suppose that in such a ballad as 'Loot' he is condoning the speaker's actions. Are we to presume that the drunkard in 'Cells' and the street girl in 'Mary, pity Women!' are projections of the author's personality? Each speaker soliloquizes on his or her experience. There is not much action; a scene, a snapshot, is presented with sharp visual imagery, in a few of the simplest words, a mental reaction to a situation, not a narrative of events. There is almost no politics or philosophy. What the proletarian soldier, rootless in India as in London, thought of war and empire is here displayed in working-class language, the aspect of Kipling's art that made so profound an effect upon Berthold Brecht in *Mother Courage* and *The Threepenny Opera*. It is Rudyard Kipling, not Bertolt Brecht, who says in more than one ballad 'Make love not war'.

While Kipling enables us to share the experience of Tommy Atkins, the traditional British soldier, all the evidence he allows is what the soldier said, so that the incomplete story leaves much to our imagination. We shall hear no more and must make the best of what we are told.

In his essay on the 'Three voices of poetry', T. S. Eliot distinguished between 'the voice of the poet talking to himself, the voice of the poet addressing an audience, and the voice of a poet when he attempts to create a dramatic character in verse', when he is keeping 'within the limits of one imaginary character addressing another imaginary character'. This line of thought led Eliot to Browning's *Dramatic Romances*, and so leads me to the relation between Browning and Kipling, with which Eliot heartily concurred. Kipling was a lifelong admirer of Browning, whose style he sometimes imitated or parodied. Both the stories and the verses of the phase in his art which we are now considering make repeated use of the structure of Browning's *Dramatic Lyrics* and *Romances*. The composition, the plan of 'My Last Duchess', or 'The Bishop Orders His Tomb', reappears in many of the barrack-room ballads, the recurrent features being that the drama is incomplete, involving a soliloquy by one speaker who tells only what he knows, and perhaps not all of that; it is addressed to a silent listener whose presence is felt though he says nothing, or very little, and is not described; and there is a third party who does not appear but who dominates the scene, perhaps a dead person. We, the audience, are drawn into the drama, identifying ourselves in sympathy, horror or even disgust with the silent listener more than with the speaker, who may be as unpleasing a personality as 'Mr Sludge the Medium', or as the unnamed rogue in 'Loot'. In a few of the ballads the monologue is extended into a dialogue by the introduction of a chorus as, in 'Danny Deever', the 'Files-on-Parade', or the messenger of death in 'Soldier, Soldier': but these secondary characters merely 'feed' the protagonist with questions or comments.

Three other influences upon Rudyard Kipling, in addition to that of Robert Browning, will be readily identified: first the Bible and the hymn book. Like most of his generation, he had been brought up in a world that read the Bible, if no other book, and sang hymns if they read no other poetry. Elementary education for the English masses had begun in the Sunday schools. The first ballad in this book contains a rather ribald quotation from the Psalms, and the last is written in the style of a hymn, with many biblical echoes. The more serious Kipling became, the more the lessons of his Calvinist childhood emerged to dominate his thinking and his style; but when he felt frivolous a second influence came up, the songs and choruses of the London music halls.

Kipling was not 'musical' as the term is understood by musicians, but he had a correct ear, a fine sense of rhythm and a love for simple tunes. We know from many good witnesses that his method of composition was to pick up an air, a folk song, a hymn tune, a popular dance tune or a music hall number, sing it quietly to himself, master its rhythms, and at last make a word-pattern to fit the tune. I have thought that his versification might be more accurately rendered in musical notation than in the convention of prosody. We know that his most famous poem, 'Recessional' (not in this book) was written to the tune of 'Eternal Father, strong to save', that the chorus of 'Follow Me 'Ome' is written to Handel's 'Dead March', that 'Mandalay' was written to a popular waltz tune, and 'Shillin' a Day' to an Irish jig; but anyone with an ear can find probable origins for himself: the Cockney song, 'Knocked 'em in the Old Kent Road' in ' "Birds of Prey" March', or 'John Brown's Body' in 'Boots'. The refrains (which some critics find tiresome), tacked on to several ballads, are music hall choruses.

The fourth influence is that of the border ballads. Many of his verses on other themes, 'Tomlinson', 'M'Andrew's Hymn' and others, are written in the Scottish dialect, and he wrote some effective imitations of the Scottish ballads, such as 'The Last Rhyme of True Thomas'. In a general study of Kipling's verse this would be a major topic, but the Scottish influence is rarely felt in the 'barrack-room ballads'. The soldiers he knew best were English and Irish, beginning with the Irishman Kearney and the Londoner, Sergeant Schofield, who had been on the staff of the school he attended, and who, I suggest, gave him his earliest notions of 'Mulvaney' and 'Ortheris'.

When considering the limitations to be set upon this book, I hesitated whether to include Kipling's *Epitaphs of the War*, and decided in their favour because they are dramatic monologues. He may have borrowed the device of making all those buried in a

Introduction

war cemetery pronounce their own epitaphs from Edgar Lee Masters, whose *Spoon River Anthology* had attracted the attention of the critics about three years earlier.

THE TEXT

The text used in this book is that of the four volumes, *Barrack-Room Ballads, The Seven Seas, The Five Nations, The Years Between,* published by Methuen, with a few variants, some of which are mentioned in the notes to particular ballads. So far as I am aware, no scholar has attempted a systematic study of the revisions that Kipling made in his verse. On the whole, as he has told us in *Something of Myself,* it was his custom in maturity to revise every sentence he wrote with scrupulous care, before committing it to print. He 'mouthed over' his ballads until he was satisfied that they sounded right, and then left them alone; he was a forward-looking man. This treatment cannot have been given, however, to his juvenile pieces which were sometimes dashed off in an afternoon to fill an odd column in his newspaper.

The first series of barrack-room ballads had been singing themselves in his head for about a year before he published them in the *Scots Observer* with its keenly critical editor. I have collated the texts as first printed in 1890 with the *Sussex Edition* which Kipling personally supervised in the last months of his life, and I find almost no textual changes. A very few modifications were made in his Cockney spelling, always in the direction of orthodoxy, and apparently for the sake of euphony. Other verses that he wrote for the *Scots Observer* at the same time received more rigorous attention.

Few textual difficulties have arisen in editing the 'barrack-room ballads'. Apart from changes in spelling, the texts of these ballads stand constant through all the respectable editions, and variants usually turn out on investigation to be due to the carelessness of editors or printers. It would be a laborious and perhaps thankless task to collate the original texts of the later ballads, some of which first appeared in journals long since defunct, and in widely separated countries.

KIPLING'S USE OF DIALECT

Whether using standard English or dialect, most of Kipling's characters are given a distinctive manner of speech which he indicates by vocabulary and word order. Most of the ballads are spoken in the first person and in the London vernacular ('Cockney'), but with great variation in style. Some, like 'Oonts' (No. 8) are put in the mouth of a speaker so illiterate as to be almost unintelligible; others, like 'Sappers' (No. 29) are merely colloquial and not far from standard English; a distinction that was not noticed by Richard le Gallienne, who wrote, in the first full criticism of Kipling's work (1899), that 'Mandalay' (No. 19) was the best of these ballads, 'though made of the very refuse of language'. I must begin by recalling that strangely little attention had been given by scholars at that date (or indeed has yet been given in 1972) to the London vernacular, as a regional dialect worthy of notice.

In his first story of barrack life ('The Three Musketeers', March 1887) Kipling made his Irishman, Mulvaney, his Yorkshireman, Learoyd, and his Londoner, Ortheris, talk appropriately, using local words, grammatical forms, and sounds rendered in an amateur phonetic spelling that was already conventional. Mulvaney's Irish brogue harked back to the eighteenth century, and had been spoken by Thackeray's Mrs O'Dowd in *Vanity Fair*. Learoyd's north-country speech was not unlike that of Tennyson's 'northern farmer'; but Ortheris introduced a new dialect into serious literature. As Peter Keating demonstrates, in his *Working Classes in Victorian Literature* (1971), Kipling was the first writer to use the London vernacular for other than comic effect. Chronologically he heads the list of those who started a vogue for 'tales of mean streets' in the 1890s, the earliest being his 'Record of Badalia Herodsfoot' (*Harper's Magazine*, November 1890). His Cockney ballads preceded those of Albert Chevalier, who intro-

Introduction

duced pathos into his songs of low life. It was this innovation that confounded the judgement of Le Gallienne, when he assumed that it was unworthy of English literature to write of love and death in such a lingo.

It is generally agreed that standard spoken English emerged from the dialects of London and the south-east in the fifteenth century and was standardized by the influence of the court and the universities; the spelling of English was fixed a little later by the custom of the printing presses. Formerly writers had spelt by ear and, as H. C. Wyld has shown, many of the forms of pronunciation that we regard as Cockney vulgarisms were in general use before printing was invented, that is, judging by the variety of spelling in manuscripts. The new vowel sounds that differentiate English from other European languages were acquiring their modern value, and the south-eastern English were already dropping their initial aitches. In the age of printing, literate persons tended to spell by eye rather than by ear, a tendency which still prevails in the days of universal education, as anyone whose memory runs back fifty years can recall. Accordingly, the literate style began to deviate from the illiterate, urged on by the grammarians with the massive support of Samuel Johnson, whose rule was that 'the most elegant speakers deviate least from the written word'. Standard English thus split on lines of class. At one end of the town, the 'correct' speakers pronounced what they read; at the other end, the 'vulgar' herd retained their traditional pronunciation, woefully misusing the newfangled French and Latin words that kept on coming in.

Walker's *Pronouncing Dictionary* (1791) contains the first analysis of Cockney speech, with the first allusion to aitch-dropping as a London error. Shakespeare's Londoners do not noticeably drop their aitches, nor does Dickens's Sam Weller.

Why is it that the Celtic and Teutonic peoples of Northern and Atlantic Europe give full value to the letter *h*, whereas the Greeks, Italians and French tend to eliminate it? In France, the letter *h* was lost in speech though retained in spelling before the Norman

Conquest, so that they brought to England a great confusion about aitch-dropping which survives to this day. It was made worse after the Renaissance when many new French words were introduced and pronounced in a frenchified mode by fashionable people. It was then the gentry who dropped their aitches, as in the words 'heir', 'hour', 'honour' to this day. A hundred years ago there were many others. Uriah Heep's ''umble' was not a vulgar Cockneyism but a misguided attempt to talk genteelly. He was behind the fashion when the linguistic reformers were trying to put back the aitches that the affected people of fashion dropped. So the extremes of upper-class and lower-class modes of speech coincided.

In both cases, aitch-dropping was borrowed from France. The unlettered millions of south-east Britain obeyed the law, whatever it was, that made their French neighbours drop their aitches while the Scotch-English, the Welsh-English, the Irish-English and the American-English did not, and do not.

A conventional standard version of Cockney speech took shape in the 1830s, and was used by many humorous writers of the Victorian age, owing its widest success to the new popular entertainment provided by the music halls, which specialized in Cockney humour. Comedians spoke or sang in the broadest London vernacular, for London working-class audiences, whose liveliness and humour responded to jokes against themselves. The London dialect thus came to be regarded as a vehicle for farce and comedy only, with the consequence that it was dismissed by the philologists as a mere misuse of language. As late as 1896, Dr Joseph Wright in his great *Dialect Dictionary* did not allow the existence of a London dialect; and in 1909 a report on The Teaching of English in London Elementary Schools described it as 'a modern corruption without legitimate credentials . . . unworthy of being the speech of any person in the capital of the Empire'. This mood of contempt is well studied in *Cockney, Past and Present*, by W. M. Matthews (1938) except that, oddly, he does not mention Kipling.

Attempts by the half-educated to avoid vulgar errors of speech

Introduction

led to the phenomenon of overreaction. In an effort to avoid the Cockney "am-an'-eggs" they said 'ham-and-heggs'. Similarly if the East End calls a rose a 'rowse', using the broad Cockney vowel, the West End feels obliged to call it a 'rewse'. Vulgar English has always betrayed itself with intrusive consonants. In Victorian English it was the intrusive *h*, which Kipling uses most sparingly (there is one in 'Mandalay'). This too is not often heard today, when the common solecism is the intrusive *r* ("The very idear of it!') which most of our broadcasting announcers affect.

The similarity between sound changes in standard French and Cockney English may be summarized in the English verb 'hurt' with its participle, 'hurting', and the French verb from which it is derived, 'heurter', with its participle 'heurtant'. In standard Scottish, 'hurting' is pronounced as it is spelt with full value for every letter; in standard English, the letter *r* modifies the vowel sound but is otherwise unheard; in Cockney English, the initial *h*, and the final *g* are dropped and the word is pronounced 'u(r)tin'. In standard French likewise 'heurtant' is pronounced 'eu(r)tan' with modified vowel sounds and with the first and last letters dropped.

In 'Mandalay', which we may select as one of Kipling's most technically perfect ballads, his soldier entirely eliminates initial *h*s and final *g*s, and slurs over the unaccented connecting words ('useter', 'thinks o' me'); he uses some irregular verbal forms ('seed' for 'saw', 'shove' for 'shoved'): double negatives ('No! you won't 'eed nothin' else!'); a few vowel sounds from conventional Cockney ('yaller', 'git', 'wot', 'arf'); euphemisms for the taboo adjectives ('plucky', 'whacking', 'blasted'). The greatest liberty he takes with language is the graphic phrase, 'Lookin' lazy', which, in later editions, he also used in the first line.

For examples of the disjunctive pronoun, another gallicism, we must search elsewhere, for example in 'Chant-Pagan' (No. 55): 'Me that 'ave seen', '*Moi qui a vu* . . .'

In 'Danny Deever' (No. 16), the aspirated aitch is used with selective skill. It is retained, indeed emphasized, for the horrific

17

key word, 'Hanging', while dropped from unaccented or insignificant words. 'They 'ave 'alted Danny Deever by 'is coffin', 'coffin' being the keyword of that line. 'Danny Deever' is an early ballad, and four years later, in 'Follow me 'Ome' (No. 35), Kipling was even more sure of his effects.

> There was no one like 'im, 'Orse or Foot,
> Nor any o' the Guns I knew.

The old army phrase, ''Orse, Foot and Guns' requires a swinging rhythm, which would be destroyed if the initial *h*s and the final *f* were replaced. In the key phrase 'Follow me 'ome', the glottal stop is sufficient to separate the open vowels; indeed it is almost stronger than an aspirate. The danger to the rhythm here is that, without the glottal stop, a vulgar reciter might ruin the line with an intrusive 'y': 'Follow me (y)ome!'

The reader of these ballads soon picks up the regular dialectal forms, which present little difficulty. A few variants are mentioned in the notes which, however, are mainly concerned with explaining technical terms, army slang, the pidgin-Hindustani that the soldiers loved to talk, or allusions to forgotten historical events.

As an example of Kipling's later ballad style the reader blest with a good ear may consider 'Lichtenstein' (No. 49) which, with no unusual words, no strange constructions, no irregular spellings, gives the effect of the Sydney-side Australian accent simply by cadence and rhythm.

Taboo Words

The publication of blasphemous or obscene expressions has long been a misdemeanour at English common law, with the consequence that certain words have been excluded, by custom, from polite conversation. Since this subject is a matter of controversy today (1973), I need say no more than that the taboo on improper language was much stronger seventy years ago. Among the suppressed words, there were two which were condemned respectively as blasphemous and obscene, for reasons which now seem irrational.

Introduction

The adjective 'bloody', which Shakespeare frequently uses in the extended sense of 'blood-thirsty', 'tending to violence', came to mean 'violent' and, like 'frightful' or 'terrible', at last became a mere emphatic, 'extremely'. Dryden had already used it in the phrase 'bloody drunk'. The reformers of 'correct' English excluded it from polite speech and, later, condemned it by a false etymology; it was supposed, on no evidence at all, to be derived from a blasphemous oath, 'By'r Lady' or 'By God's blood'. For over a century it remained underground, though the commonest of all emphatics among the impolite classes, until partially released as a joke in Shaw's *Pygmalion* (1912). Meanwhile it had been concealed behind several euphemisms, such as 'blooming', 'bleeding' or even 'hairy' (see note 1), which are used in Kipling's Cockney ballads and stories.

The history of 'bugger', derived from the Norman-French 'bougre', is even more strange. The French brought it back from the Fourth Crusade, where they had met barbarous Bulgarians who, though Christian, were heretics; and heretics in the age of faith were often credited with unnatural vices. In French and English alike, a 'bougre' or 'bugger' meant a rough, uncouth, chap or bloke, with a suppressed secondary sense, implied by a wink or nod, that he might be a practising homosexual. The two meanings were kept distinct and there was no doubt which you meant, though both were excluded from polite English conversation. Since Londoners tended to pronounce 'bugger' and 'beggar' very much alike, with thickened 'obscure' vowels, it was easy to write down 'beggar' when every reader knew you meant 'bugger' in its innocent sense, a chap or bloke. Even then, it was slightly contemptuous, condescending. Englishmen never said with respect that a man was a 'good bugger' as Americans say a 'good guy'.

KIPLING AND THE ARMY

The strength of the British Empire lay in sea power and oceanic trade, all depending upon the Royal Navy, a ubiquitous peace-keeping force, which secured the seaways of the world without fighting a fleet action between Navarino (1827) and Jutland (1916). On the other hand, the army was very small for so huge an empire, with one-third of the manpower of the French army and one-sixth of that of Russia, these two being the comparable imperial states. The British army was strictly professional and class-conscious; its officers were exclusively 'gentlemen', giving their loyalty directly to the crown; the rank and file were drawn from the unskilled labourers, and recruiting was good when employment was bad. All armies live by *esprit de corps*, the comradeship of men who are willing to live and die together. Perhaps no army since the Roman legions has had so strong a sense of regimental unity as the old British regular army, or so strong a sense of loyalty.

The first ballad in this series was written in the fifty-third year of Queen Victoria's reign and the twentieth of her widowhood, so that all serving soldiers had spent their whole lives under her rule, and few would remember her as anything but a secluded widow. Her Golden Jubilee in 1887 had been a festival of empire and her Diamond Jubilee in 1897 was to raise her repute still higher. Perhaps the most successful constitutional monarch in history, the queen belonged to the people, not to the aristocracy, and her longevity contributed to her prestige. The faint murmurs of criticism that were heard did not come from the masses but from those of the rich and great who envied her remote grandeur. Without an effort she played them off the stage. The respect of the people might be tinged with sardonic humour as in this ballad, but it was the kind of humour that goes with true affection.

As known to Kipling, the army was in many respects undergoing a reformation which had been begun in 1871 by Gladstone through his secretary for war, Cardwell, and was carried further in 1881 by the completion of the linked battalion system. Each regiment was to have one battalion ready for active service and probably stationed in India or the Mediterranean, while the other battalion was recruiting or training 'at home'. The officers were now selected by examination and trained at military colleges, and the

Introduction

private men, who had formerly enlisted for the whole of their active life, were replaced by short-term men who followed the drum for seven years before returning to civil life as reservists who could be recalled to the colours in a national emergency. Kipling's stories and ballads teem with allusions to the old long-service soldiers who were rather contemptuous of the new short-service men.

Much remained to be done in modernizing and civilizing the army, in this progressive generation, when new means of communication and transportation, new discoveries and inventions, new weapons of war sprang up every year, quite changing the character of human life. The old army which fought in the Crimea much as it had fought under Wellington wore scarlet coats, carried handloaded, short-range rifles (having only just moved on from 'Brown Bess' muskets), manœuvred in mass or column, stood shoulder to shoulder in line to destroy the enemy with pointblank volleys, or formed squares bristling with bayonets to defy cavalry charges. They had been unbeatable in the field, if properly handled. It was at Balaclava, on 25 October 1854, that the war correspondent W. H. Russell watched the scarlet-clad double line of the 93rd Highlanders standing firm against the Russian cavalry, a 'thin red streak' across the battlefield, afterwards more memorably described as a 'thin red line of heroes'. In Kipling's day the marching regiments spoke of themselves as 'linesmen' and the 'Widow's uniform' was still scarlet.

But in those days, however, there was little advantage for the European soldier over the Sudanese or Afghan tribesman if it came to close quarters on rough ground. Until the 1880s the British military memory had several sore spots, when 'savages' like the Zulus at Isandhlwana, the Sudanese at Tamai or the Afghans at Maiwand had beaten 'civilized men' in fair fight; but this happened rarely after 1890. Modern weapons of war prevailed. The 'Martini' breechloading rifle of the 1880s with its long-range accuracy, and the far better 'Lee-Metford' rifle of the 1890s with its mechanical reloading and smokeless powder, turned every infantryman into a sharpshooter. Volley-firing and close formations vanished. Soldiers in action now 'took open order' and lay down to shoot individually. The change took time. Some years were needed for re-equipment and training; there were, as there always are, oldfashioned seniors who mistrusted change, and there were occasions, as at the battle of Omdurman in 1898, when close-order tactics were still effective. But broadly speaking we may say that Wolseley's victory over the Egyptian nationalists at Tel-el-Kebir in 1882 was the last British battle fought in the old style, with scarlet coats and volleys in close order. Thereafter troops wore khaki for protective coloration, and fought individually in extended lines.

It was Wolseley, caricatured by W. S. Gilbert as 'the modern major-general', who seemed to be 'England's only soldier'. Having fought in several campaigns with great efficiency, he revised the training, equipment and tactics of the army in spite of persistent obstruction from the Treasury which was unwilling to spend public money on so unpopular a cause as army reform. The army, and the soldiers, were disliked. Even more obstructive was the 'establishment' of senior officers led by the queen's cousin, the old Duke of Cambridge. Successful at the active end of the army, Wolseley was unable to overrule conservatism at the top and not until after the Boer War was the higher command itself modernized in time for 1914.

More important than training and equipment was the moral and physical welfare of the soldiers. Everyone knows that their systematic medical care was initiated by Florence Nightingale during the Crimean War, but what could be done for the army in India when the art of living in the tropics was so little understood? The clothing, diet and domestic habit of the soldiers were grossly unsuitable. Drunkenness and venereal disease were widespread; it was not yet known that cholera was waterborne or that mosquitoes carried malaria; there was no refrigeration nor airconditioning. The private soldiers had few rational amusements. For the most part, these virile young men were obliged by the conditions

Introduction

of service to live as bachelors, sleeping on cots in barrack rooms as bare as oldfashioned school dormitories. Only a few married quarters were provided for senior men of proved good conduct. Their wives, 'married on the strength', followed the drum as untrained nurses and washerwomen.

The soldiers' hero was not Wolseley, but Sir Frederick Roberts, afterwards Lord Roberts ('Bobs'), the Commander-in-Chief in India, who had won the VC as a young officer and lived to command victorious armies in Afghanistan and South Africa. It was 'Bobs' who devoted forty years to the promotion of the soldiers' welfare, and changed the reckless, drunken scapegraces described in Kipling's early ballads into the literate wellbehaved soldiers of 1914.

This small band of expensive professionals was deployed on the exposed frontier of the empire in the Middle East, the potential enemy being Russia. After the reorganization of 1871 there were no British regular troops in the new 'White Dominions' and only a few small detachments at strategic points, that is to say naval stations in some colonies. In many colonies there were no British soldiers at all, though this is not the impression you would receive from recent popular accounts of the empire. The navy was responsible for defending the seaways.

For more than 100 years British strategic policy had been chiefly concerned with frustrating the Russian advance into the territories of the dissolving Turkish empire. Russia's age-long search for an outlet to 'warm-water' oceans, through the Black Sea into the Mediterranean or through the Persian Gulf into the Arabian Sea, was checked at every point by British sea power; and the last stand against Russian penetration of all central Asia must be on the north-west frontier of India. On two occasions which have a curious resemblance, in 1839–42 and in 1878–80, aggressive British governments had adopted a forward policy with the intention of securing Afghanistan as a 'buffer-state' between the Russian and the British empires. In each instance the British intervened imprudently in a civil war, whereupon the Afghans united against the invaders; in each war there were humiliating defeats and fruitless victories; in each the Afghans maintained their independence. It was these wars that the old soldiers were talking about while the young reporter, Kipling, applied an attentive eye and ear.

Meanwhile the tribal territory between the Indus River and the Afghan frontier remained in a state of lawlessness. The inhabitants were Sunni Moslems, known to the troops as Pathans ('paythans'), who had never been controlled by the former Sikh or Afghan rulers and lived by raiding the peaceful inhabitants across the border. Hence the military barrier known as the North-West Frontier along which for 100 years a British-Indian army of about six divisions was always mobilized. Their function was strategic, to deter Russian aggression, but from year to year they found themselves engaged in defensive operations or in reprisals against the Pathan tribes. All professional British soldiers expected a tour of duty on 'the Frontier' where they would get some acquaintance with active service, and critics hinted that the army liked things that way since the Frontier made a battle-training ground. Nine-tenths of the British-Indian army was deployed there or in the cities along its line of communications, while scores of millions in southern India enjoyed unbroken peace for four generations, and rarely saw a British soldier.

There were other imperial wars while Kipling was in the East; in Burma, which he visited only as a steamship passenger, and in the Sudan, of which he had no personal knowledge. His informant on the Egyptian campaigns seems to have been his schoolfriend 'Stalky', Major-General L. C. Dunsterville, who had served at Suakin in the Red Sea. Years later when the Boer War broke out Kipling was spending the winter in Cape Town as a guest of Cecil Rhodes, his close friend. Early in 1900 he twice visited the battlefields, and it would have surprised his innumerable admirers to know that this was the first time he had seen troops under fire. He was in Bloemfontein through an epidemic of enteric fever, then neither preventable nor curable beyond what nursing could do.

Introduction

It swept through the armies and a year later devastated the refugee camps where the isolated women and children from the battle area were collected.

The Boer War (as it was always called) was not a 'colonial' campaign like those on the Indian and Egyptian frontiers, but regular warfare between European combatants who were equally well armed.

The Boers (now known as Afrikaners) had used the wealth of the gold mines to purchase German fieldguns and Mauser rifles, and no one doubted that their stubborn courage would make them formidable. Contrary to the accepted myth, it was they who attacked the small British garrison in superior numbers, crossing the frontier, besieging three British towns, Kimberley, Ladysmith and Mafeking, and inflicting humiliating defeats on three isolated columns in British territory. The Black Week of December 1899 when these mishaps occurred caused more dismay among the readers of the sensational press than among the soldiers, who had not yet deployed their full strength. Lord Roberts arrived early in 1900 with an adequate force, with Kitchener as his chief-of-staff and, in a single campaign, swept the Boer armies off the field, occupying the two Boer capitals. He then went home, supposing the war to be over.

Kitchener, who had been left to wind up the campaign with a much reduced force, found himself faced with a national guerilla rising, the first of many which have defied great regular armies in this century. With ruthless administrative measures and little bloodshed, Kitchener crushed the Boer guerrillas in eighteen months, bringing them to total surrender, a rare event indeed in military history. It was Kitchener the soldier, and not Milner the civil high commissioner, who dictated generous terms to the defeated Boers, holding out to them hopes of self-government as soon as the reconstruction should be complete. The war had several unusual features. In spite of their stubborn resistance, the Boers were not good haters. The soldiers on both sides respected and even nourished a sort of affection for one another, as is evident

25

in several of Kipling's ballads. There were no deliberate atrocities in this war, and hating your enemy was left to the stay-at-home civilians. The one chance of a Boer victory had been to enlist support from foreign nations or from rebels in other colonies; they got neither. Canadians, Australians, New Zealanders and British South Africans volunteered to fight for the empire, as did many thousands of British men of all classes. Hence the title of Kipling's book, *The Five Nations*. A more remarkable fact is that this was a white man's war. The Indian army was not employed, and the warlike black tribes of South Africa stood neutral, hardly yet politically conscious and unaware of their fate. For if the British won the war, the Boers won the peace, and it was the racial policy of Kruger that was to prevail in South Africa, as the world knows today.

The Boer War broke out at a moment when weapons had reached a high degree of efficiency while movement of stores still depended upon horses and mules. No mechanical transport was yet in mass production, and off the railways armies moved on foot at two and a half miles an hour. This gap between killing power and mobility provided a moment when mounted infantry, who rode to the battle on horseback but dismounted to fight on foot, were the most useful arm (see 'M.I.', No. 48). Kitchener's toughest problems were to convert his townbred soldiers into horsemen, and to provide the horses, thousands of them bought from the Argentine. The Boers, born frontiersmen, came naturally to this roving life, as did the British 'colonials', but it was strange to the Cockneys. Twelve years later, in the next war, the automobile put mounted infantry out of business.

Similarly, the 15-pounder field guns, firing mostly shrapnel which burst with a sensitive timefuse at long range, were still drawn by teams of six horses as they had been 100 years earlier. Several of these ballads (No. 3, No. 11, No. 32) require some understanding of the ways of horsed artillery.

The ammunition was carried in heavy two-wheeled carts, limbers, which were linked together in pairs, for jolting across

Introduction

rough ground. The guns were also linked to a limber, trail first, that is with muzzles pointing backwards. The team of six horses was arranged in pairs with a driver (more properly a ride-and-driver) on each nearside (left-hand) horse. The leading driver, in charge of the gun, was a bombardier (equivalent to a corporal in the infantry). On coming into action the guns 'wheel into line', that is, turn right round so that the guns face the enemy. The teams are then unhooked and ridden away to the rear. This, and the similar moment of bringing up the teams to change ground, were the moments of greatest danger, when the guns could neither shoot nor move: the old soldier in No. 3 compares the guns man-handled around with their trails in the air to fine ladies of the 1880s holding up their 'bustles', the exaggerated trains of their skirts, as they turn to settle in a chair.

The Royal Horse Artillery, so-called because every man rode a horse whereas in the Field Artillery half the gun team had a rough ride on the limbers, were the *corps d'élite*, armed with lighter guns, 13-pounders after about 1890, which could gallop with the cavalry. (See 'The Jacket', No. 32.)

For mountain warfare in the 1880s and 1890s a popular weapon was the 7-pounder 'screw-gun' (No. 7) which could be rapidly unscrewed into three pieces for carriage, with its two wheels, on the backs of five mules. Screw-guns could go almost anywhere that men could go.

The Boer War was the last war fought by the British in which, to use the soldiers' grim phrase, the doctor's bill was longer than the butcher's bill. Hitherto, all armies had been decimated by camp fevers which could neither be prevented nor cured. It was only in the 1890s, after Koch's discovery of the cholera bacillus (1883) and Ross's identification of the malarial mosquito (1897) that control of these diseases, and later of typhoid, could be begun. By 1914 they were largely held in check.

I Barrack-Room Ballads

(from Barrack-Room Ballads and Other Verses, 1892)

To T.A.

I have made for you a song,
And it may be right or wrong,
But only you can tell me if it's true;
I have tried for to explain
Both your pleasure and your pain,
And, Thomas, here's my best respects to you.

O there'll surely come a day
When they'll give you all your pay,
And treat you as a Christian ought to do;
So, until that day comes round,
Heaven keep you safe and sound,
And, Thomas, here's my best respects to you!

R.K.

1 *The Widow at Windsor*

'Ave you 'eard o' the Widow at Windsor
  With a hairy gold crown on 'er 'ead?
She 'as ships on the foam—she 'as millions at 'ome,
  An' she pays us poor beggars in red.
    (Ow, poor beggars in red!)
There's 'er nick on the cavalry 'orses,
  There's 'er mark on the medical stores—
An' 'er troopers you'll find with a fair wind be'ind
  That takes us to various wars.
    (Poor beggars!—barbarious wars!)
      Then 'ere's to the Widow at Windsor,
        An' 'ere's to the stores an' the guns,
      The men an' the 'orses what makes up the forces
        O' Missis Victorier's sons.
      (Poor beggars! Victorier's sons!)

Walk wide o' the Widow at Windsor,
  For 'alf o' Creation she owns:
We 'ave bought 'er the same with the sword an' the flame,
  An' we've salted it down with our bones.
    (Poor beggars!—it's blue with our bones!)
Hands off o' the sons o' the Widow,
  Hands off o' the goods in 'er shop,
For the Kings must come down an' the Emperors frown
  When the Widow at Windsor says 'Stop'!
    (Poor beggars!—we're sent to say 'Stop'!)
      Then 'ere's to the Lodge o' the Widow,
        From the Pole to the Tropics it runs—
      To the Lodge that we tile with the rank an' the file,
        An' open in form with the guns.
      (Poor beggars!—it's always they guns!)

Tommy

We 'ave 'eard o' the Widow at Windsor.
    It's safest to let 'er alone:
For 'er sentries we stand by the sea an' the land
    Wherever the bugles are blown.
        (Poor beggars! – an' don't we get blown!)
Take 'old o' the Wings o' the Mornin',
    An' flop round the earth till you're dead;
But you won't get away from the tune that they play
    To the bloomin' old rag over'ead.
        (Poor beggars! – it's 'ot over'ead!)
            Then 'ere's to the sons o' the Widow,
                Wherever, 'owever they roam.
            'Ere's all they desire, an' if they require
                A speedy return to their 'ome.
        (Poor beggars! – they'll never see 'ome!)

2 Tommy

I went into a public-'ouse to get a pint o' beer,
The publican 'e up an' sez, 'We serve no red-coats here.'
The girls be'ind the bar they laughed an' giggled fit to die,
I outs into the street again an' to myself sez I:
            O it's Tommy this, an' Tommy that, an'
                'Tommy, go away';
            But it's 'Thank you, Mister Atkins, when the
                band begins to play,
            The band begins to play, my boys, the band begins
                to play,
            O it's 'Thank you, Mister Atkins,' when the band
                begins to play.

I went into a theatre as sober as could be,
They gave a drunk civilian room, but 'adn't none for me;
They sent me to the gallery or round the music-'alls,
But when it comes to fightin, Lord! they'll shove me in
    the stalls!
                For it's Tommy this, an' Tommy that, an'
                    'Tommy, wait outside';
                But it's 'Special train for Atkins' when the
                    trooper's on the tide,
                The troopship's on the tide, my boys, the
                    troopship's on the tide,
                O it's 'Special train for Atkins' when the trooper's
                    on the tide

Yes, makin' mock o' uniforms that guard you while you sleep
Is cheaper than them uniforms, an' they're starvation cheap;
An' hustlin' drunken soldiers when they're going' large a bit
Is five times better business than paradin' in full kit.
                Then it's Tommy this, an' Tommy that,
                    an' 'Tommy, 'ow's yer soul?'
                But it's 'Thin red line of 'eroes' when the drums
                    begin to roll.
                The drums begin to roll, my boys, the drums begin
                    to roll,
                O it's 'Thin red line of 'eroes' when the drums
                    begin to roll.

We aren't no thin red 'eroes, nor we aren't no
    blackguards too,
But single men in barricks, most remarkable like you;
An' if sometimes our conduck isn't all your fancy paints,
Why, single men in barricks don't grow into plaster saints;
                While it's Tommy this, an' Tommy that, an'
                    'Tommy, fall be'ind,'

32

But it's 'Please to walk in front, sir,' when there's
 trouble in the wind,
There's trouble in the wind, my boys, there's
 trouble in the wind,
O it's 'Please to walk in front, sir,' when there's
 trouble in the wind.

You talk o' better food for us, an' schools, an' fires, an' all:
We'll wait for extry rations if you treat us rational;
Don't mess about the cook-room slops, but prove it to
 our face
The Widow's Uniform is not the soldier-man's disgrace.
  For it's Tommy this, an' Tommy that, an'
   'Chuck him out, the brute!'
  But it's 'Saviour of 'is country' when the guns
   begin to shoot;
  An' it's Tommy this, an' Tommy that, an'
   anything you please;
  An' Tommy ain't a bloomin' fool – you bet that
   Tommy sees!

3 *The Young British Soldier*

When the 'arf-made recruity goes out to the East
'E acts like a babe an' 'e drinks like a beast,
An' 'e wonders because 'e is frequent deceased
 Ere 'e's fit for to serve as a soldier.
  Serve, serve, serve as a soldier,
  Serve, serve, serve as a soldier,
  Serve, serve, serve as a soldier,
   So-oldier *of* the Queen!

Now all you recruities what's drafted to-day,
You shut up your rag-box an' 'ark to my lay.
An' I'll sing you a soldier as far as I may:
    A soldier what's fit for a soldier.
        Fit, fit, fit for a soldier . . .

First mind you steer clear o' the grog-sellers' huts,
For they sell you Fixed Bay'nets that rots out your guts —
Ay, drink that 'ud eat the live steel from your butts —
    An' it's bad for the young British Soldier.
        Bad, bad, bad for the soldier . . .

When the cholera comes — as it will past a doubt —
Keep out of the wet and don't go on the shout,
For the sickness gets in as the liquor dies out,
    An' it crumples the young British soldier.
        Crum-, crum-, crumples the soldier . . .

But the worst o' your foes is the sun over'ead:
You *must* wear your 'elmet for all that is said:
If 'e finds you uncovered 'e'll knock you down dead,
    An' you'll die like a fool of a soldier.
        Fool, fool, fool of a soldier . . .

If you're cast for fatigue by a sergeant unkind,
Don't grouse like a woman nor crack on nor blind;
Be handy and civil, and then you will find
    That it's beer for the young British soldier
        Beer, beer, beer for the soldier . . .

Now, if you must marry, take care she is old —
A troop-sergeant's widow's the nicest I'm told,
For beauty won't help if your rations is cold,
    Nor love ain't enough for a soldier.
        'Nough, 'nough, 'nough for a soldier . . .

The Young British Soldier

If the wife should go wrong with a comrade, be loth
To shoot when you catch 'em — you'll swing, on my oath! —
Make 'im take 'er and keep 'er: that's Hell for them both,
    An' you're shut o' the curse of a soldier.
        Curse, curse, curse of a soldier . . .

When first under fire an' you're wishful to duck,
Don't look nor take 'eed at the man that is struck,
Be thankful you're livin', and trust to your luck
    And march to your front like a soldier.
        Front, front, front like a soldier . . .

When 'arf of your bullets fly wide in the ditch,
Don't call your Martini a cross-eyed old bitch;
She's human as you are — you treat her as sich,
    An' she'll fight for the young British soldier.
        Fight, fight, fight for the soldier . . .

When shakin' their bustles like ladies so fine,
The guns o' the enemy wheel into line,
Shoot low at the limbers an' don't mind the shine,
    For noise never startles the soldier
        Start-, start-, startles the soldier . . .

If your officer's dead and the sergeants look white,
Remember it's ruin to run from a fight:
So take open order, lie down, and sit tight,
    And wait for supports like a soldier.
        Wait, wait, wait like a soldier . . .

When you're wounded and left on Afghanistan's plains,
And the women come out to cut up what remains,
Jest roll to your rifle and blow out your brains
    An' go to your Gawd like a soldier.
        Go, go, go like a soldier,
        Go, go, go like a soldier,
        Go, go, go like a soldier,
          So-oldier *of* the Queen!

4 *Belts*

There was a row in Silver Street that's near to Dublin Quay,
Between an Irish regiment an' English cavalree;
It started at Revelly an' it lasted on till dark:
The first man dropped at Harrison's, the last forninst the Park.
      For it was: – 'Belts, belts, belts, an' that's one for you!'
      An' it was 'Belts, belts, belts, an' that's done for you!'
      O buckle an' tongue
      Was the song that we sung
      From Harrison's down to the Park!

There was a row in Silver Street – the regiments was out,
They called us 'Delhi Rebels,' an' we answered 'Threes about!'
That drew them like a hornet's nest – we met them good an' large,
The English at the double an' the Irish at the charge.
      Then it was: – 'Belts . . .

There was a row in Silver Street – an' I was in it too;
We passed the time o' day, an' then the belts went whirraru!
I misremember what occurred, but subsequint the storm
A *Freeman's Journal Supplemint* was all my uniform.
      O it was: – 'Belts . . .

There was a row in Silver Street – they sent the Polis there,
The English were too drunk to know, the Irish didn't care;
But when they grew impertinint we simultaneous rose,
Till half o' them was Liffey mud an' half was tatthered clo'es.
      For it was: – 'Belts . . .

There was a row in Silver Street – it might ha' raged till now,
But some one drew his side-arm clear, an' nobody knew how;
'Twas Hogan took the point an' dropped; we saw the red blood run:
An' so we all was murderers that started out in fun.
      While it was: – 'Belts . . .

There was a row in Silver Street — but that put down the shine,
Wid each man whisperin 'to his next: ' 'Twas never work o' mine!'
We went away like beaten dogs, an' down the street we bore him,
The poor dumb corpse that couldn't tell the bhoys were sorry
    for him.
        When it was: — 'Belts . . .

There was a row in Silver Street — it isn't over yet,
For half of us are under guard wid punishments to get;
'Tis all a merricle to me as in the Clink I lie:
There was a row in Silver Street — begod, I wonder why!
        But it was: — 'Belts, belts, belts, an' that's one for you!'
        An' it was 'Belts, belts, belts, an' that's done for you!'
        O buckle an' tongue
        Was the song that we sung
        From Harrison's down to the Park!

5 *Cells*

I've a head like a concertina: I've a tongue like a button-stick:
I've a mouth like an old potato, and I'm more than a little sick,
But I've had my fun o' the Corp'ral's Guard: I've made the
    cinders fly,
And I'm here in the Clink for a thundering drink and blacking the
    Corporal's eye.

  With a second-hand overcoat under my head,
    And a beautiful view of the yard,
O it's pack-drill for me and a fortnight's C.B.
    For 'drunk and resisting the Guard!'
    Mad drunk and resisting the Guard —
    'Strewth, but I socked it them hard!
So it's pack-drill for me and a fortnight's C.B.
    For 'drunk and resisting the Guard.'

I started o' canteen porter, I finished o' canteen beer,
But a dose o' gin that a mate slipped in, it was that that brought
    me here.
'Twas that and an extry double Guard that rubbed my nose in
    . the dirt;
But I fell away with the Corp'ral's stock and the best of the
    Corp'ral's shirt.

I left my cap in a public-house, my boots in the public road,
And Lord knows where, and I don't care, my belt and my
    tunic goed;
They'll stop my pay, they'll cut away the stripes I used to wear,
But I left my mark on the Corp'ral's face, and I think he'll keep
    it there!

My wife she cries on the barrack-gate, my kid in the barrack-yard,
It ain't that I mind the Ord'ly room – it's *that* that cuts so hard.
I'll take my oath before them both that I will sure abstain,
But as soon as I'm in with a mate and gin, I know I'll do it again!

    With a second-hand overcoat under my head,
    And a beautiful view of the yard,
Yes, it's pack-drill for me and a fortnight's C.B.
    For 'drunk and resisting the Guard!'
    Mad drunk and resisting the Guard –
    'Strewth, but I socked it them hard!
So it's pack-drill for me and a fortnight's C.B.
    For 'drunk and resisting the Guard.'

Route Marchin'

6 Route Marchin'

We're marchin' on relief over Injia's sunny plains,
A little front o' Christmas-time an' just be'ind the Rains;
Ho! get away you bullock-man, you've 'eard the bugle blowed,
There's a regiment a-comin' down the Grand Trunk Road;
> With its best foot first
> And the road a-sliding past,
> An' every bloomin' campin'-ground exactly like the last;
> While the Big Drum says,
> With 'is *rowdy-dowdy-dow!*' –
> '*Kiko kissywarsti* don't you *hamsher argy jow?*'[1]

Oh, there's them Injian temples to admire when you see,
There's the peacock round the corner an' the monkey up the tree,
An' there's that rummy silver-grass a-wavin' in the wind,
An' the old Grand Trunk a-trailin' like a rifle-sling be'ind.
> While it's best foot first, . . .

At half-past five's Revelly, an' our tents they down must come,
Like a lot of button-mushrooms when you pick 'em up at 'ome.
But it's over in a minute, an' at six the column starts,
While the women and the kiddies sit an' shiver in the carts.
> An' it's best foot first, . . .

Oh, then it's open order, an' we lights our pipes an' sings,
An' we talks about our rations an' a lot of other things,
An' we thinks o' friends in England, an' we wonders what
they're at,
An' 'ow they would admire for to hear us sling the *bat*.[2]
> An' it's best foot first, . . .

[1] 'Why don't you get on?'
[2] Language. Thomas's first and firmest conviction is that he is a profound Orientalist and a fluent speaker of Hindustani. As a matter of fact, he depends largely on the sign language.

It's none so bad o' Sunday, when you're lyin' at your ease,
To watch the kites a-wheelin' round them feather-'eaded trees,
For although there ain't no women, yet there ain't no barrick-
    yards,
So the orficers goes shootin' an' the men they plays at cards.
        Till it's best foot first, . . .

So 'ark an' 'eed, you rookies, which is always grumblin' sore,
There's worser things than marchin' from Umballa to Cawnpore;
An' if your 'eels are blistered an' they feels to 'urt like 'ell,
You drop some tallow in your socks an' that will make 'em well.
        For it's best foot first, . . .

We're marchin' on relief over Injia's coral strand,
Eight 'undred fightin' Englishmen, the Colonel, and the Band;
Ho! get away you bullock-man, you've 'eard the bugle blowed,
There's a regiment a-comin' down the Grand Trunk Road;
            With its best foot first
            And the road a-sliding past,
            An' every bloomin' campin'-ground exactly like the last;
            While the Big Drum says,
            With 'is *'rowdy-dowdy-dow!'* –
        'Kiko kissywarsti don't you *hamsher argy jow?'*

7 *Screw-Guns*

Smokin' my pipe on the mountings, sniffin' the mornin'-cool,
I walks in my old brown gaiters along o' my old brown mule,
With seventy gunners be'ind me, an' never a beggar forgets
It's only the pick of the Army that handles the dear little pets –
        'Tss! 'Tss!

Screw-Guns

For you all love the screw-guns — the screw-guns they
    all love you!
So when we call round with a few guns, o' course you
    will know what to do — hoo! hoo!
Jest send in your Chief an' surrender — it's worse if you
    fights or you runs:
You can go where you please, you can skid up the trees,
    but you don't get away from the guns!

They sends us along where the roads are, but mostly we goes where
    they ain't:
We'd climb up the side of a sign-board an' trust to the stick o' the
    paint:
We've chivied the Naga an' Looshai, we've give the Afreedeeman
    fits,
For we fancies ourselves at two thousand, we guns that are built
    in two bits — 'Tss! 'Tss!
        For you all love the screw-guns . . .

If a man doesn't work, why, we drills 'im an' teaches 'im 'ow to
    behave;
If a beggar can't march, why, we kills 'im an' rattles 'im into 'is
    grave.
You've got to stand up to our business an' spring without snatchin'
    or fuss.
D'you say that you sweat with the field-guns? By God, you must
    lather with us — 'Tss! 'Tss!
        For you all love the screw-guns . . .

The eagles is screamin' around us, the river's a-moanin' below,
We're clear o' the pine an' the oak-scrub, we're out on the rocks an'
    the snow,
An' the wind is as thin as a whip-lash what carries away to the
    plains

The rattle an' stamp o' the lead-mules – the jinglety jink o' the
chains – 'Tss! 'Tss!
    For you all love the screw-guns . . .

There's a wheel on the Horns o' the Mornin', an' a wheel on the
edge o' the Pit,
An' a drop into nothin' beneath you as straight as a beggar can spit:
With the sweat runnin' out o' your shirt-sleeves, an the sun off
the snow in your face,
An' 'arf o' the men on the drag-poles to hold the old gun in 'er
place – 'Tss! 'Tss!
    For you all love the screw-guns . . .

Smokin' my pipe on the mountings, sniffin' the mornin'-cool,
I climbs in my old brown gaiters along o' my old brown mule.
The monkey can say what our road was – the wild-goat 'e knows
where we passed.
Stand easy, you long-eared old darlin's! Out drag-ropes! With
shrapnel! Hold fast – 'Tss! 'Tss!
      For you all love the screw-guns – the screw-guns they
        all love you!
      So when we take tea with a few guns, o' course you will
        know what to do – hoo! hoo!
      Jest send in your Chief an' surrender – it's worse if you
        fights or you runs:
      You may hide in the caves, they'll be only your graves,
        but you can't get away from the guns!

8 Oonts

(NORTHERN INDIA TRANSPORT TRAIN)

Wot makes the soldier's 'eart to penk, wot makes 'im to perspire?
It isn't standin' up to charge nor lyin' down to fire;
But it's everlastin' waitin' on a everlastin' road
For the commissariat camel an' 'is commissariat load.
   O the oont,[1] O the oont, O the commissariat oont!
     With 'is silly neck a-bobbin' like a basket full o' snakes;
   We packs 'im like an idol, an' you ought to 'ear 'im grunt,
     An' when we gets 'im loaded up 'is blessed girth-rope breaks.

Wot makes the rear-guard swear so 'ard when night is drorin' in,
An' every native follower is shiverin' for 'is skin?
It ain't the chanst o' being rushed by Paythans from the 'ills,
It's the commissariat camel puttin' on 'is bloomin' frills!
   O the oont, O the oont, O the hairy scary oont!
     A-trippin' over tent-ropes when we've got the night alarm!
   We socks 'im with a stretcher-pole an' 'eads 'im off in front,
     An' when we've saved 'is bloomin life'? 'e chaws our
       bloomin' arm.

The 'orse 'e knows above a bit, the bullock's but a fool,
The elephant's a gentleman, the battery-mule's a mule;
But the commissariat cam-u-el, when all is said an' done,
'E's a devil an' a ostrich an' a orphan-child in one.
   O the oont, O the oont, O the Gawd-forsaken oont!
     The lumpy-'umpy 'ummin'-bird a-singin' where 'e lies,
   'E's blocked the whole division from the rear-guard to the front,
     An' when we get him up again – the beggar goes an' dies!

---

[1] Camel:—*oo* is pronounced like *u* in 'bull', but by Mr Atkins to rhyme with 'front'.

'E'll gall an' chafe an' lame an' fight – 'e smells most awful vile;
'E'll lose 'isself for ever if you let 'im stray a mile;
'E's game to graze the 'ole day long an' 'owl the 'ole night through,
An' when 'e comes to greasy ground 'e splits 'isself in two.
   O the oont, O the oont, O the floppin', droppin' oont!
     When 'is long legs give from under an' 'is meltin' eye is dim,
    The tribes is up be'ind us, and the tribes is out in front –
     It ain't no jam for Tommy, but it's kites an' crows for 'im.

So when the cruel march is done, an' when the roads is blind,
An' when we sees the camp in front an' 'ears the shots be'ind.
Ho! then we strips 'is saddle off, and all 'is woes is past:
'E thinks on us that used 'im so, and gets revenge at last.
   O the oont, O the oont, O the floatin', bloatin' oont!
    The late lamented camel in the water-cut 'e lies;
  We keeps a mile be'ind 'im an' we keeps a mile in front,
    But 'e gets into the drinkin'-casks, and then o' course we dies.

9 *The Widow's Party*

'Where have you been this while away,
    'Johnnie, Johnnie?'
Out with the rest on a picnic lay,
    Johnnie, my Johnnie, aha!
They called us out of the barrack-yard
To Gawd knows where from Gosport Hard,
And you can't refuse when you get the card,
    And the Widow gives the party.
     (*Bugle:* Ta – rara – ra-ra-rara!)

44

The Widow's Party

'What did you get to eat and drink,
     'Johnnie, Johnnie?'
Standing water as thick as ink,
     Johnnie, my Johnnie, aha!
A bit o' beef that were three year stored,
A bit o' mutton as tough as a board,
And a fowl we killed with a sergeant's sword,
     When the Widow give the party.

'What did you do for knives and forks,
     'Johnnie, Johnnie?'
We carries 'em with us wherever we walks,
     Johnnie, my Johnnie, aha!
And some was sliced and some was halved,
And some was crimped and some was carved,
And some was gutted and some was starved,
     When the Widow give the party.

'What ha' you done with half your mess,
     'Johnnie, Johnnie?'
They couldn't do more and they wouldn't do less,
     Johnnie, my Johnnie, aha!
They ate their whack and they drank their fill,
And I think the rations has made them ill,
For half my comp'ny's lying still
     Where the Widow give the party.

'How did you get away – away,
     'Johnnie, Johnnie?'
On the broad o' my back at the end o' the day,
     Johnnie, my Johnnie, aha!
I comed away like a bleedin' toff,
For I got four niggers to carry me off,
As I lay in the bight of a canvas trough,
     When the Widow give the party.

'What was the end of all the show,
          'Johnnie, Johnnie?'
Ask my Colonel, for I don't know,
          Johnnie, my Johnnie, aha!
We broke a King and we built a road –
A court-house stands where the reg'ment goed.
And the river's clean where the raw blood flowed
          When the Widow give the party.
          (*Bugle:* Ta – rara – ra-ra-rara!)

10 *Gentlemen-Rankers*

To the legion of the lost ones, to the cohort of the damned,
     To my brethren in their sorrow overseas,
Sings a gentleman of England cleanly bred, machinely crammed,
     And a trooper of the Empress, if you please.
Yes, a trooper of the forces who has run his own six horses,
     And faith he went the pace and went it blind,
And the world was more than kin while he held the ready tin,
     But to-day the Sergeant's something less than kind.
          We're poor little lambs who've lost our way,
               Baa! Baa! Baa!
          We're little black sheep who've gone astray,
               Baa – aa – aa!
          Gentlemen-rankers out on the spree,
          Damned from here to Eternity,
          God ha' mercy on such as we,
               Baa! Yah! Bah!

Oh, it's sweet to sweat through stables, sweet to empty kitchen slops,
     And it's sweet to hear the tales the troopers tell,
To dance with blowzy housemaids at the regimental hops
     And thrash the cad who says you waltz too well.

46

Gentlemen-Rankers

Yes, it makes you cock-a-hoop to be 'Rider' to your troop,
  And branded with a blasted worsted spur,
When you envy, O how keenly, one poor Tommy being cleanly
  Who blacks your boots and sometimes calls you 'Sir.'

If the home we never write to, and the oaths we never keep,
  And all we know most distant and most dear,
Across the snoring barrack-room return to break our sleep,
  Can you blame us if we soak ourselves in beer?
When the drunken comrade mutters and the great guard-lantern
    gutters
  And the horror of our fall is written plain,
Every secret, self-revealing on the aching white-washed ceiling,
  Do you wonder that we drug ourselves from pain?

We have done with Hope and Honour, we are lost to Love and
    Truth,
  We are dropping down the ladder rung by rung,
And the measure of our torment is the measure of our youth.
  God help us, for we knew the worst too young!
Our shame is clean repentance for the crime that brought the
    sentence,
  Our pride it is to know no spur of pride,
And the Curse of Reuben holds us till an alien turf enfolds us
  And we die, and none can tell Them where we died.
    We're poor little lambs who've lost our way,
      Baa! Baa! Baa!
    We're little black sheep who've gone astray,
      Baa — aa — aa!
    Gentlemen-rankers out on the spree,
    Damned from here to Eternity.
    God ha' mercy on such as we,
      Baa! Yah! Bah!

47

11 'Snarleyow'

This 'appened in a battle to a batt'ry of the corps
Which is first among the women an' amazin' first in war;
An' what the bloomin' battle was I don't remember now,
But Two's off-lead 'e answered to the name o' *Snarleyow*.
     Down in the Infantry, nobody cares;
     Down in the Cavalry, Colonel 'e swears;
     But down in the lead with the wheel at the flog
     Turns the bold Bombardier to a little whipped dog!

They was movin' into action, they was needed very sore,
To learn a little schoolin' to a native army corps,
They 'ad nipped against an uphill, they was tuckin' down the brow,
When a tricky, trundlin' roundshot give the knock to *Snarleyow*.

They cut 'im loose an' left 'im – 'e was almost tore in two –
But he tried to follow after as a well-trained 'orse should do;
'E went an' fouled the limber, an' the Driver's Brother squeals:
'Pull up, pull up for *Snarleyow* – 'is head's between 'is 'eels!'

The Driver 'umped 'is shoulder, for the wheels was goin' round,
An' there ain't no 'Stop, conductor!' when a batt'ry's changin'
    ground;
Sez 'e: 'I broke the beggar in, an' very sad I feels,
'But I couldn't pull up, not for *you* – your 'ead between your 'eels!'

'E 'adn't 'ardly spoke the word, before a droppin' shell
A little right the batt'ry an' between the sections fell;
An' when the smoke 'ad cleared away, before the limber wheels,
There lay the Driver's Brother with 'is 'ead between 'is 'eels.

Ford o' Kabul River

Then sez the Driver's Brother, an' 'is words was very plain,
'For Gawd's own sake get over me, an' put me out o' pain.'
They saw 'is wounds was mortial, an' they judged that it was best,
So they took an' drove the limber straight across 'is back an' chest.

The Driver 'e give nothin' 'cept a little coughin' grunt,
But 'e swung 'is 'orses 'andsome when it came to 'Action Front!'
An' if one wheel was juicy, you may lay your Monday head
'Twas juicier for the niggers when the case began to spread.

The moril of this story, it is plainly to be seen:
You 'avn't got no families when servin' of the Queen —
You 'avn't got no brothers, fathers, sisters, wives, or sons —
If you want to win your battles take an' work your bloomin' guns!
    Down in the Infantry, nobody cares;
    Down in the Cavalry, Colonel 'e swears;
    But down in the lead with the wheel at the flog
    Turns the bold Bombardier to a little whipped dog!

12 Ford o' Kabul River

  Kabul town's by Kabul river —
    Blow the bugle, draw the sword —
  There I lef' my mate for ever,
    Wet an' drippin' by the ford.
  Ford, ford, ford o' Kabul river,

    Ford o' Kabul river in the dark!
  There's the river up and brimmin', an
    there's 'arf a squadron swimmin'
  'Cross the ford o' Kabul river in the dark.

Kabul town's a blasted place –
  Blow the bugle, draw the sword –
'Strewth I shan't forget 'is face
  Wet an' drippin' by the ford!
    Ford, ford, ford o' Kabul river,
      Ford o' Kabul river in the dark!
    Keep the crossing-stakes beside you, an' they
      will surely guide you
      'Cross the ford o' Kabul river in the dark.

Kabul town is sun and dust –
  Blow the bugle, draw the sword –
I'd ha' sooner drowned fust
  'Stead of 'im beside the ford.
    Ford, ford, ford o' Kabul river,
      Ford o' Kabul river in the dark!
    You can 'ear the 'orses threshin'; you can
      'ear the men a-splashin',
      'Cross the ford o' Kabul river in the dark.

Kabul town was ours to take –
  Blow the bugle, draw the sword –
I'd ha' left it for 'is sake –
  'Im that left me by the ford.
    Ford, ford, ford o' Kabul river,
      Ford o' Kabul river in the dark!
    It's none so bloomin' dry there; ain't you
      never comin' nigh there,
      'Cross the ford o' Kabul river in the dark?

Kabul town'll go to hell –
  Blow the bugle, draw the sword –
'Fore I see him 'live an' well –
  'Im the best beside the ford.

Gunga Din

Ford, ford, ford o' Kabul river,
   Ford o' Kabul river in the dark!
Gawd 'elp 'em if they blunder, for their
   boots'll pull 'em under,
   By the ford o' Kabul river in the dark.

Turn your 'orse from Kabul town —
   Blow the bugle, draw the sword —
'Im an' 'arf my troop is down,
   Down an' drownded by the ford.
   Ford, ford, ford o' Kabul river,
      Ford o' Kabul river in the dark!
   There's the river low an' fallin', but it ain't
      no use o' callin'
   'Cross the ford o' Kabul river in the dark.

13 Gunga Din

You may talk o' gin and beer
When you're quartered safe out 'ere,
An' you're sent to penny-fights an' Aldershot it;
But when it comes to slaughter
You will do your work on water,
An' you'll lick the bloomin' boots of 'im that's got it
Now in Injia's sunny clime,
Where I used to spend my time
A-servin' of 'Er Majesty the Queen.
Of all them blackfaced crew
The finest man I knew
Was our regimental *bhisti*, Gunga Din.

He was 'Din! Din! Din!
'You limpin' lump o' brick-dust, Gunga Din!
'Hi! slippery *hitherao*!
'Water, get it! *Panee lao*![1]
You squidgy-nosed old idol, Gunga Din.'

The uniform 'e wore
Was nothin' much before,
An' rather less than 'arf o' that be'ind,
For a piece o' twisty rag
An' a goatskin water-bag
Was all the field-equipment 'e could find.
When the sweatin' troop-train lay
In a sidin' through the day,
Where the 'eat would make your bloomin' eyebrows crawl,
We shouted 'Harry By!'[2]
Till our throats were bricky-dry,
Then we wopped 'im 'cause 'e couldn't serve us all.
          It was 'Din! Din! Din!
     'You 'eathen, where the mischief 'ave you been?
          'You put some *juldee*[3] in it
          'Or I'll *marrow*[4] you this minute
     'If you don't fill up my helmet, Gunga Din.'

'E would dot an' carry one
Till the longest day was done;
An' 'e didn't seem to know the use o' fear.
If we charged or broke or cut,
You could bet your bloomin' nut,
'E'd be waitin' fifty paces right flank rear.
With 'is mussick[5] on 'is back,
'E would skip with our attack,

[1] Bring water swiftly.
[2] Mr Atkins's equivalent for 'O brother'.   [3] Be quick.
[4] Hit you.   [5] Water-skin.

Gunga Din

An' watch us till the bugles made 'Retire,'
An' for all 'is dirty 'ide
'E was white, clear white, inside
When 'e went to tend the wounded under fire!
            It was 'Din! Din! Din!'
      With the bullets kickin' dust-spots on the green.
            When the cartridges ran out,
                  You could hear the front-files shout,
      'Hi! ammunition-mules an' Gunga Din!'

I shan't forgit the night
When I dropped be'ind the fight
With a bullet where my belt-plate should 'a' been.
I was chokin' mad with thirst,
An' the man that spied me first
Was our good old grinnin', gruntin' Gunga Din.
'E lifted up my 'ead,
An' he plugged me where I bled,
An' 'e guv me 'arf-a-pint o' water-green:
It was crawlin' and it stunk,
But of all the drinks I've drunk,
I'm gratefullest to one from Gunga Din.
            It was 'Din! Din! Din!
      'Ere's a beggar with a bullet through 'is spleen;
            ''E's chawin' up the ground,
                  'An' 'e's kickin' all around:
      'For Gawd's sake git the water, Gunga Din!'

'E carried me away
To where a dooli lay,
An' a bullet come an' drilled the beggar clean.
'E put me safe inside,
An' just before 'e died,
'I 'ope you liked your drink,' sez Gunga Din.

So I'll meet 'im later on
At the place where 'e is gone —
Where it's always double drill and no canteen;
'E'll be squattin' on the coals
Givin' drink to poor damned souls,
An' I'll get a swig in hell from Gunga Din!
   Yes, Din! Din! Din!
  You Lazarushian-leather Gunga Din.
    Though I've belted you and flayed you,
    By the livin' Gawd that made you,
  You're a better man than I am, Gunga Din.

14 'Fuzzy-Wuzzy'

(SOUDAN EXPEDITIONARY FORCE)

We've fought with many men acrost the seas,
 An' some of 'em was brave an' some was not:
The Paythan an' the Zulu an' Burmese;
 But the Fuzzy was the finest o' the lot.
We never got a ha'porth's change of 'im:
 'E squatted in the scrub an' 'ocked our 'orses,
'E cut our sentries up at Sua*kim*,
 An' 'e played the cat an' banjo with our forces.
   So 'ere's *to* you, Fuzzy-Wuzzy, at your 'ome in the
    Soudan;
   You're a pore benighted 'eathen but a first-class
    fightin' man;
   We gives you your certificate, an' if you want it
    signed
   We'll come an' 'ave a romp with you whenever
    you're inclined.

'Fuzzy-Wuzzy'

We took our chanst among the Kyber 'ills,
  The Boers knocked us silly at a mile,
The Burman give us Irriwaddy chills,
  An' a Zulu *impi* dished us up in style:
But all we ever got from such as they
  Was pop to what the Fuzzy made us swaller;
We 'eld our bloomin' own, the papers say,
  But man for man the Fuzzy knocked us 'oller.
        Then 'ere's *to* you, Fuzzy-Wuzzy, an' the missis
            and the kid;
        Our orders was to break you, an' of course we
            went an' did.
        We sloshed you with Martinis, an' it wasn't
            'ardly fair;
        But for all the odds agin' you, Fuzzy-Wuz, you
            broke the square.

'E 'asn't got no papers of 'is own,
  'E 'asn't got no medals nor rewards,
So we must certify the skill 'e's shown
  In usin' of 'is long two-'anded swords:
When 'e's 'oppin' in an' out among the bush
  With 'is coffin-'eaded shield an' shovel-spear,
An 'appy day with Fuzzy on the rush
  Will last an 'ealthy Tommy for a year.
        So 'ere's *to* you, Fuzzy-Wuzzy, an' your
            friends which are no more,
        If we 'adn't lost some messmates we would
            'elp you to deplore;
        But give an' take's the gospel, an' we'll call
            the bargain fair,
        For if you 'ave lost more than us, you
            crumpled up the square!

55

'E rushes at the smoke when we let drive,
　　An', before we know, 'e's 'ackin' at our 'ead;
'E's all 'ot sand an' ginger when alive,
　　An' 'e's generally shammin' when 'e's dead.
'E's a daisy, 'e's a ducky, 'e's a lamb!
　　'E's a injia-rubber idiot on the spree,
'E's the on'y thing that doesn't give a damn
　　For a Regiment o' British Infantree!
　　　　　So 'ere's *to* you, Fuzzy-Wuzzy, at your 'ome
　　　　　　in the Soudan;
　　　　　You're a pore benighted 'eathen but a first-
　　　　　　class fightin' man;
　　　　　An' 'ere's *to* you, Fuzzy-Wuzzy, with your
　　　　　　'ayrick 'ead of 'air –
　　　　　You big black boundin' beggar – for you broke
　　　　　　a British square!

15 Loot

If you've ever stole a pheasant-egg be'ind the
　　keeper's back,
　　If you've ever snigged the washin' from the line,
If you've ever crammed a gander in your bloomin'
　　'aversack,
　　You will understand this little song o' mine.
But the service rules are 'ard, an' from such we
　　are debarred,
　　For the same with English morals does not suit.
　　(*Cornet:* Toot! toot!)
W'y, they call a man a robber if 'e stuffs 'is marchin'
　　clobber
　　With the –

Loot

(*Chorus*) Loo! loo! Lulu! lulu! Loo! loo! Loot!
  loot! loot!
  Ow the loot!
  Bloomin' loot!
  That's the thing to make the boys git up
  an' shoot!
  It's the same with dogs an' men,
  If you'd make 'em come again
  Clap 'em forward with a Loo! loo! Lulu!
  Loot!
  (*ff*) Whoopee! Tear 'im, puppy! Loo! loo!
  Lulu! Loot! loot! loot!

If you've knocked a nigger edgeways when 'e's
  thrustin' for your life,
  You must leave 'im very careful where 'e fell;
An' may thank your stars an' gaiters if you didn't
  feel 'is knife
  That you ain't told off to bury 'im as well.
Then the sweatin' Tommies wonder as they spade
  the beggars under
  Why lootin' should be entered as a crime;
So if my song you'll 'ear, I will learn you plain an'
  clear
  'Ow to pay yourself for fightin' overtime.
  (*Chorus*) With the loot, . . .

Now remember when you're 'acking round a gilded
  Burma god
  That 'is eyes is very often precious stones;
An' if you treat a nigger to a dose o' cleanin'-rod
  'E 's like to show you everything 'e owns.
When 'e won't prodooce no more, pour some water
  on the floor

Where you 'ear it answer 'ollow to the boot
  (*Cornet:* Toot! toot!) –
When the ground begins to sink, shove your baynick
    down the chink,
  An' you're sure to touch the –
(*Chorus*) Loo! loo! Lulu! Loot! loot! loot!
      Ow the loot! . . .

When from 'ouse to 'ouse you're 'unting, you must
    always work in pairs –
  It 'alves the gain, but safer you will find –
For a single man gets bottled on them twisty-wisty
    stairs,
  An' a woman comes and clobs 'im from be'ind.
When you've turned 'em inside out, an' it seems
    beyond a doubt
  As if there weren't enough to dust a flute
    (*Cornet:* Toot! toot!) –
Before you sling your 'ook, at the 'ousetops take a look,
  For it's underneath the tiles they 'ide the loot.
    (*Chorus*) Ow the loot! . . .

You can mostly square a Sergint an' a Quartermaster
    too,
  If you only take the proper way to go;
I could never keep my pickin's, but I've learned
    you all I knew –
  An' don't you never say I told you so.
An' now I'll bid good-bye, for I'm gettin' rather dry,
  An' I see another tunin' up to toot
    (*Cornet:* Toot! toot!) –
So 'ere's good-luck to those that wears the Widow's
    clo'es,

An' the Devil send 'em all they want o' loot!
   (*Chorus*) Yes, the loot,
           Bloomin' loot!
  In the tunic an' the mess-tin an' the boot!
    It's the same with dogs an' men,
    If you'd make 'em come again
(*fff*) Whoop 'em forward with a Loo! loo! Lulu!
    Loot! loot! loot!
  Heeya! Sick 'im, puppy! Loo! loo! Lulu!
    Loot! loot! loot!

16 Danny Deever

'What are the bugles blowin' for?' said Files-on-Parade.
'To turn you out, to turn you out,' the Colour-Sergeant
    said.
'What makes you look so white, so white?' said Files-on-
    Parade.
'I'm dreadin' what I've got to watch,' the Colour-Sergeant
    said.
        For they're hanging' Danny Deever, you can
           hear the Dead March play,
        The regiment's in 'ollow square – they're hangin'
           him to-day;
        They've taken of his buttons off an' cut his
           stripes away,
        An' they're hangin' Danny Deever in the
           mornin'.

'What makes the rear-rank breathe so 'ard?' said Files-on-
    Parade.
'It's bitter cold, it's bitter cold,' the Colour-Sergeant said.
'What makes that front-rank man fall down? says
    Files-on-Parade.

'A touch o' sun, a touch o' sun,' the Colour-Sergeant said.
  They are hangin' Danny Deever, they are
   marchin' of 'im round,
  They 'ave 'alted Danny Deever by 'is coffin on
   the ground;
  An' 'e'll swing in 'arf a minute for a sneakin'
   shootin' hound –
  O they're hangin' Danny Deever in the mornin'!

' 'Is cot was right-'and cot to mine,' said Files-on-Parade.
' 'E's sleepin' out an' far tonight,' the Colour-Sergeant said.
'I've drunk 'is beer a score o' times,' said Files-on-Parade.
' 'E's drinkin' bitter beer alone,' the Colour-Sergeant said.
  They are hangin' Danny Deever, you must
   mark 'im to 'is place,
  For 'e shot a comrade sleepin' – you must look
   'im in the face;
  Nine 'undred of 'is county an' the regiment's
   disgrace,
  While they're hangin' Danny Deever in the
   mornin'.

'What's that so black agin the sun? said Files-on-Parade.
'It's Danny fightin' 'ard for life,' the Colour-Sergeant said.
'What's that that whimpers over'ead?' said Files-on-Parade.
'It's Danny's soul that's passin' now,' the Colour-Sergeant
 said.
  For they're done with Danny Deever, you can
   'ear the quickstep play,
  The regiment's in column, an' they're marchin'
   us away;
  Ho! the young recruits are shakin', an' they'll
   want their beer today,
  After hangin' Danny Deever in the mornin'.

17 Troopin'

(OUR ARMY IN THE EAST)

Troopin', troopin', troopin' to the sea:
'Ere's September come again — the six-year men are free.
O leave the dead be'ind us, for they cannot come away
To where the ship's a-coalin' up that takes us 'ome to-day.
  We're goin' 'ome, we're goin' 'ome,
   Our ship is at the shore,
  An' you must pack your 'aversack,
   For we won't come back no more.
  Ho, don't you grieve for me,
   My lovely Mary-Ann,
  For I'll marry you yit on a fourp'ny bit
   As a time-expired man.

The Malabar's in 'arbour with the Jumner at 'er tail,
An' the time-expired's waitin' of 'is orders for to sail.
Ho! the weary waitin' when on Khyber 'ills we lay,
But the time-expired's waitin' of 'is orders 'ome to-day.

They'll turn us out at Portsmouth wharf in cold an' wet
  an' rain,
All wearin' Injian cotton kit, but we will not complain;
They'll kill us of pneumonia — for that's their little way —
But damn the chills and fever, men, we're goin' 'ome
  to-day!

Troopin', troopin', winter's round again!
See the new draf's pourin' in for the old campaign;

61

Ho, you poor recruities, but you've got to earn your
    pay –
What's the last from Lunnon, lads? We're goin' there
    to-day.

Troopin', troopin', give another cheer –
'Ere's to English women an' a quart of English beer.
The Colonel an' the regiment an' all who've got to stay,
Gawd's mercy strike 'em gentle – Whoop! we're goin'
    'ome to-day.
> We're goin' 'ome, we're goin' 'ome,
>   Our ship is at the shore,
> An' you must pack your 'aversack,
>   For we won't come back no more.
> Ho, don't you grieve for me,
>   My lovely Mary-Ann,
> For I'll marry you yit on a fourp'ny bit
>   As a time-expired man.

18 Soldier, Soldier

'Soldier, soldier come from the wars,
'Why don't you march with my true love?'
'We're fresh from off the ship an' 'e's maybe give
    the slip,
'An' you'd best go look for a new love.'

> New love! True love!
> Best go look for a new love,
> The dead they cannot rise, an' you'd better
>   dry your eyes,
> An' you'd best go look for a new love.

Soldier, Soldier

'Soldier, soldier come from the wars,
'What did you see o' my true love?'
'I seed 'im serve the Queen in a suit o' rifle-green,
'An' you'd best go look for a new love.'

'Soldier, soldier come from the wars,
'Did ye see no more o' my true love?'
'I seed 'im runnin' by when the shots begun to fly –
But you'd best go look for a new love.'

'Soldier, soldier come from the wars,
'Did aught take 'arm to my true love?'
'I couldn't see the fight, for the smoke it lay so white –
'An' you'd best go look for a new love.'

'Soldier, soldier come from the wars,
'I'll up an' tend to my true love!'
' 'E's lying on the dead with a bullet through 'is 'ead,
'An' you'd best go look for a new love.'

'Soldier, soldier come from the wars,
'I'll down an' die with my true love!'
'The pit we dug 'll 'ide 'im an' the twenty men
        beside 'im –
'An' you'd best go look for a new love.

'Soldier, soldier come from the wars,
'Do you bring no sign from my true love?'
'I bring a lock of 'air that 'e allus used to wear
'An' you'd best go look for a new love.'

63

'Soldier, soldier come from the wars,
'O then I know it's true I've lost my true love!'
'An' I tell you truth again — when you've lost the feel
    o' pain
'You'd best take me for your true love.'

        True love! New love!
        Best take 'im for a new love,
        The dead they cannot rise, an' you'd better
            dry your eyes,
        An' you'd best take 'im for your true love.

19 Mandalay

By the old Moulmein Pagoda, lookin' eastward to
    the sea,
There's a Burma girl a-settin', and I know she thinks
    o' me;
For the wind is in the palm-trees, and the temple-bells
    they say:
'Come you back, you British soldier; come you back to
    Mandalay!'
        Come you back to Mandalay,
        Where the old Flotilla lay:
        Can't you 'ear their paddles chunkin' from
            Rangoon to Mandalay?
        On the road to Mandalay,
        Where the flyin'-fishes play,
        An' the dawn comes up like thunder outer
            China 'crost the Bay!

Mandalay

'Er petticoat was yaller an' 'er little cap was green,
An' 'er name was Supi-yaw-lat – jes' the same as Theebaw's
    Queen,
An' I seed her first a-smokin' of a whackin' white cheroot,
An' a-wastin' Christian kisses on an 'eathen idol's foot:
        Bloomin' idol made o' mud –
        Wot they called the Great Gawd Budd –
        Plucky lot she cared for idols when I kissed 'er
           where she stud!
        On the road to Mandalay . . .

When the mist was on the rice-fields an' the sun was
    droppin' slow,
She'd git 'er little banjo an' she'd sing '*Kulla-lo-lo!*'
With 'er arm upon my shoulder an' 'er cheek agin my
    cheek
We useter watch the steamers an' the *hathis* pilin' teak.
        Elephints a-pilin' teak
        In the sludgy, squdgy creek,
        Where the silence 'ung that 'eavy you was 'arf
           afraid to speak!
        On the road to Mandalay . . .

But that's all shove be'ind me – long ago an' fur away,
An' there ain't no 'busses runnin' from the Bank to
    Mandalay;
An' I'm learnin' 'ere in London what the ten-year
    soldier tells:
'If you've 'eard the East a-callin', you won't never 'eed
    naught else.'
        No! you won't 'eed nothin' else
        But them spicy garlic smells,
        An' the sunshine an' the palm-trees an' the
           tinkly temple-bells;
        On the road to Mandalay . . .

I am sick o' wastin' leather on these gritty pavin'-stones,
An' the blasted Henglish drizzle wakes the fever in my bones;
Tho' I walks with fifty 'ousemaids outer Chelsea to the
    Strand,
An' they talks a lot o' lovin', but wot do they understand?
        Beefy face an' grubby 'and –
        Law! wot do they understand?
        I've a neater, sweeter maiden in a cleaner,
           greener land!
        On the road to Mandalay . . .

Ship me somewheres east of Suez, where the best is like
    the worst,
Where there aren't no Ten Commandments an' a man
    can raise a thirst;
For the temple-bells are callin', an' it's there that I
    would be –
By the Old Moulmein Pagoda, looking lazy at the sea;
        On the road to Mandalay,
        Where the old Flotilla lay,
        With our sick beneath the awnings when we went
           to Mandalay!
        O the road to Mandalay,
        Where the flyin'-fishes play,
        An' the dawn comes up like thunder outer
           China 'crost the Bay!

20 Shillin' a Day

My name is O'Kelly, I've heard the Revelly
From Birr to Bareilly, from Leeds to Lahore,
Hong-Kong and Peshawur,
Lucknow and Etawah,
And fifty-five more all endin' in 'pore.'
Black Death and his quickness, the depth and the thickness,
Of sorrow and sickness I've known on my way,
But I'm old and I'm nervis,
I'm cast from the Service,
And all I deserve is a shillin' a day.
    (*Chorus*) Shillin' a day,
           Bloomin' good pay –
           Lucky to touch it, a shillin' a day!

Oh, it drives me half crazy to think of the days I
Went slap for the Ghazi, my sword at my side,
When we rode Hell-for-leather
Both squadrons together,
That didn't care whether we lived or we died.
But it's no use despairin', my wife must go charin'
An' me commissairin' the pay-bills to better.
So if me you be'old
In the wet and the cold,
By the Grand Metropold won't you give me a letter?
(*Full Chorus*) Give 'im a letter –
           'Can't do no better,
           Late Troop-Sergeant-Major an' – runs with
              a letter!
           Think what 'e's been,
           Think what 'e's seen,
           Think of his pension an' –

GAWD SAVE THE QUEEN!

II Barrack-Room Ballads

(all but Nos. 31 and 36 from *The Seven Seas*, 1896)

When 'Omer smote 'is bloomin' lyre,
  He'd 'eard men sing by land an' sea;
An' what he thought 'e might require,
'E went an' took – the same as me!

The market-girls an' fishermen,
  The shepherds an' the sailors, too,
They 'eard old songs turn up again,
  But kep' it quiet – same as you!

They knew 'e stole; 'e knew they knowed.
  They didn't tell, nor make a fuss,
But winked at 'Omer down the road,
  An' 'e winked back – the same as us!

21 'Back to the Army Again'

I'm 'ere in a ticky ulster an' a broken billycock 'at,
A-layin' on to the sergeant I don't know a gun from a bat;
My shirt's doin' duty for jacket, my sock's stickin out o' my boots,
An' I'm learnin' the damned old goose-step along o' the new
    recruits!

      Back to the Army again, sergeant,
        Back to the Army again.
      Don't look so 'ard, for I 'aven't no card,
        I'm back to the Army again!

I done my six years' service. 'Er Majesty sez: 'Good day –
You'll please to come when you're rung for, an' 'ere's your 'ole
    back-pay;
An' four-pence a day for baccy – an' bloomin' gen'rous, too;
An' now you can make your fortune – the same as your
    orf'cers do.'

      Back to the Army again, sergeant,
        Back to the Army again;
      'Ow did I learn to do right-about turn?
        I'm back to the Army again!

A man o' four-an'-twenty that 'asn't learned of a trade –
Beside 'Reserve' agin' him – 'e'd better be never made.
I tried my luck for a quarter, an' that was enough for me,
An' I thought of 'Er Majesty's barricks, an' I thought I'd go
    an' see.

      Back to the Army again, sergeant,
        Back to the Army again;
      'Tisn't my fault if I dress when I 'alt –
        I'm back to the Army again!

'Back to the Army Again'

The sergeant arst no questions, but 'e winked the other eye,
'E sez to me, "Shun!' an' I shunted, the same as in days gone by;
For 'e saw the set o' my shoulders, an' I couldn't 'elp 'oldin' straight
When me 'an the other rookies come under the barrick gate.

> Back to the Army again, sergeant,
>   Back to the Army again;
> 'Oo would ha' thought I could carry an' port?
> I'm back to the Army again!

I took my bath, an' I wallered — for, Gawd, I needed it so!
I smelt the smell o' the barricks, I 'eard the bugles go.
I 'eard the feet on the gravel — the feet o' the men what drill —
An' I sez to my flutterin' 'eart-strings, I sez to 'em, 'Peace, be still!'

> Back to the Army again, sergeant,
>   Back to the Army again;
> 'Oo said I knew when the Jumner was due?
> I'm back to the Army again!

I carried my slops to the tailor; I sez to 'im, 'None o' your lip!
You tight 'em over the shoulders, an' loose 'em over the 'ip,
For the set o' the tunic's 'orrid.' An' 'e sez to me, 'Strike me dead,
But I thought you was used to the business!' an' so 'e done what
    I said.

> Back to the Army again, sergeant,
>   Back to the Army again.
> Rather too free with my fancies? Wot — me?
> I'm back to the Army again!

Next week I'll 'ave 'em fitted; I'll buy me a swagger-cane;
They'll let me free o' the barricks to walk on the Hoe again
In the name o' William Parsons, that used to be Edward Clay,
An' — any pore beggar that wants it can draw my fourpence a day!

Back to the Army again, sergeant,
   Back to the Army again:
     Out o' the cold an' the rain, sergeant,
     Out o' the cold an' the rain.

       'Oo's there?
A man that's too good to be lost you,
   A man that is 'andled an' made –
A man that will pay what 'e cost you
   In learnin' the others their trade – parade!
You're droppin' the pick o' the Army
   Because you don't 'elp 'em remain,
But drives 'em to cheat to get out o' the street
   An' back to the Army again!

22 'Birds of Prey' March

March! The mud is cakin' good about our trousies.
   Front! – eyes front, an' watch the Colour-casin's drip.
Front! The faces of the women in the 'ouses
   Ain't the kind o' things to take aboard the ship.

Cheer! An' we'll never march to victory.
Cheer! An' we'll never live to 'ear the cannon roar!
   The Large Birds o' Prey
   They will carry us away,
An you'll never see your soldiers any more!

Wheel! Oh, keep your touch; we're goin' round a corner.
   Time! – mark time, an' let the men be'ind us close.
Lord! the transport's full, an' 'alf our lot not on 'er –
   Cheer, O cheer! We're going off where no one knows.

'Birds of Prey' March

March! The Devil's none so black as 'e is painted!
　　Cheer! We'll 'ave some fun before we're put away.
'Alt, an' 'and 'er out – a woman's gone and fainted!
　　Cheer! Get on – Gawd 'elp the married men today!

Hoi! Come up, you 'ungry beggars, to yer sorrow.
　　('Ear them say they want their tea, an' want it quick!)
You won't have no mind for slingers, not to-morrow –
　　No; you'll put the 'tween-decks stove out, bein' sick!

'Alt! The married kit 'as all to go before us!
　　'Course it's blocked the bloomin' gangway up again!
Cheer, O cheer the 'Orse Guards watchin' tender o'er us,
　　Keepin' us since eight this mornin' in the rain!

Stuck in 'eavy marchin'-order, sopped and wringin' –
　　Sick, before our time to watch 'er 'eave an' fall,
'Ere's your 'appy 'ome at last, an' stop your singin'.
　　'Alt! Fall in along the troop-deck! Silence all!

Cheer! For we'll never live to see no bloomin' victory!
Cheer! An' we'll never live to 'ear the cannon roar!
　　　　(One cheer more!)
　　　The jackal an' the kite
　　　'Ave an 'ealthy appetite,
An' you'll never see your soldiers any more! ('Ip! Urroar!)
　　　The eagle an' the crow
　　　They are waitin' ever so,
An' you'll never see your soldiers any more! ('Ip! Urroar!)
　　　Yes, the Large Birds o' Prey
　　　They will carry us away,
An' you'll never see your soldiers any more!

23 The 'Eathen

The 'eathen in 'is blindness bows down to wood an' stone;
'E don't obey no orders unless they is 'is own;
'E keeps 'is side-arms awful: 'e leaves 'em all about,
An' then comes up the regiment an' pokes the 'eathen out.

> *All along o' dirtiness, all along o' mess,*
> *All along o' doin' things rather-more-or-less,*
> *All along of abby-nay[1], kul,[2] an' hazar-ho,[3]*
> *Mind you keep your rifle an' yourself jus' so!*

The young recruit is 'aughty – 'e draf's from Gawd knows where;
They bid 'im show 'is stockin's an' lay 'is mattress square;
'E calls it bloomin' nonsense – 'e doesn't know, no more –
An' then up comes 'is Company an' kicks 'im round the floor!

The young recruit is 'ammered – 'e takes it very 'ard;
'E 'angs 'is 'ead an' mutters – 'e sulks about the yard;
'E talks o' 'cruel tyrants' 'e'll swing for by-an'-by,
An' the others 'ears an' mocks 'im, an' the boy goes orf to cry.

The young recruit is silly – 'e thinks o' suicide;
'E's lost 'is gutter-devil; 'e 'asn't got 'is pride;
But day by day they kicks 'im, which 'elps 'im on a bit,
Till 'e finds 'isself one mornin' with a full an' proper kit.

> *Gettin' clear o' dirtiness, gettin' done with mess,*
> *Gettin' shut o' doin' things rather-more-or-less;*
> *Not so fond of abby-nay, kul, nor hazar-ho,*
> *Learns to keep 'is rifle an' 'isself jus' so!*

[1] Not now.   [2] Tomorrow.   [3] Wait a bit.

The 'Eathen

The young recruit is 'appy — 'e throws a chest to suit;
You see 'im grow mustaches; you 'ear 'im slap 'is boot;
'E learns to drop the 'bloodies' from every word 'e slings,
An' 'e shows an 'ealthy brisket when 'e strips for bars an' rings.

The cruel-tyrant-sergeants they watch 'im 'arf a year;
They watch 'im with 'is comrades, they watch 'im with 'is beer;
They watch 'im with the women at the regimental dance,
And the cruel-tyrant-sergeants send 'is name along for 'Lance.'

An' now 'e's 'arf o' nothin', an' all a private yet,
'Is room they up an' rags 'im to see what they will get;
They rags 'im low an' cunnin', each dirty trick they can,
But 'e learns to sweat 'is temper an' 'e learns to sweat 'is man.

An', last, a Colour-Sergeant, as such to be obeyed,
'E schools 'is men at cricket, 'e tells 'em on parade;
They sees 'em quick an' 'andy, uncommon set an' smart,
An' so 'e talks to orficers which 'ave the Core at 'eart.

'E learns to do 'is watchin' without it showin' plain;
'E learns to save a dummy, an' shove 'im straight again;
'E learns to check a ranker that's buyin' leave to shirk;
An' 'e learns to make men like 'im so they'll learn to like their work.

An' when it comes to marchin' he'll see their socks are right,
An' when it comes to action 'e shows 'em 'ow to sight,
'E knows their ways of thinkin' and just what's in their mind;
'E knows when they are takin' on an' when they've fell be'ind.

'E knows each talkin' corpril that leads a squad astray;
'E feels 'is innards 'eavin', 'is bowels givin' way;
'E sees the blue-white faces all tryin' 'ard to grin,
An' 'e stands an' waits an' suffers till it's time to cap 'em in.

An' now the hugly bullets come peckin' through the dust,
An' no one wants to face 'em, but every beggar must;
So, like a man in irons which isn't glad to go,
They moves 'em off by companies uncommon stiff an' slow.

Of all 'is five years' schoolin' they don't remember much
Excep' the not retreatin', the step an' keepin' touch.
It looks like teachin' wasted when they duck an' spread an' 'op,
But if 'e 'adn't learned 'em they'd be all about the shop!

An' now it's "Oo goes backward?' an' now it's "Oo comes on?'
And now it's 'Get the doolies,' an' now the captain's gone;
An' now it's bloody murder, but all the while they 'ear
'Is voice, the same as barrick drill, a-shepherdin' the rear.

'E's just as sick as they are, 'is 'eart is like to split,
But 'e works 'em, works 'em, works 'em till he feels 'em take
        the bit;
The rest is 'oldin' steady till the watchful bugles play,
An' 'e lifts 'em, lifts 'em, lifts 'em through the charge that wins
        the day!

> The 'eathen in 'is blindness bows down to wood an' stone;
> 'E don't obey no orders unless they is 'is own;
> The 'eathen in 'is blindness must end where 'e began,
> But the backbone of the Army is the non-commissioned man!
>
> Keep away from dirtiness – keep away from mess,
> Don't get into doin' things rather-more-or-less!
> Let's ha' done with abby-nay, kul and hazar-ho;
> Mind you keep your rifle and yourself jus' so!

24 'The Men that fought at Minden'

A SONG OF INSTRUCTION

The men that fought at Minden, they was rookies in
    their time –
  So was them that fought at Waterloo!
All the 'ole command, yuss, from Minden to Maiwand,
  They was once dam' sweeps like you!

    Then do not be discouraged, 'Eaven is your 'elper,
      We'll learn you not to forget;
    An' you mustn't swear an' curse, or you'll only catch
      it worse,
    For we'll make you soldiers yet!

The men that fought at Minden, they 'ad stocks beneath
    their chins,
  Six inch 'igh an' more;
But fatigue it was their pride, and they *would* not be
    denied
  To clean the cook-'ouse floor.

The men that fought at Minden, they had anarchistic
    bombs
  Served to 'em by name of 'and-grenades;
But they got it in the eye (same as you will by an' by)
  When they clubbed their field-parades.

The men that fought at Minden, they 'ad buttons up an'
    down,
  Two-an'-twenty dozen of 'em told;
But they didn't grouse an' shirk at an hour's extry work,
  They kept 'em bright as gold.

The men that fought at Minden, they was armed with
    musketoons,
  Also, they was drilled by 'alberdiers;
I don't know what they were, but the sergeants took
    good care
  They washed be'ind their ears.

The men that fought at Minden, they 'ad ever cash
    in 'and
  Which they did not bank nor save,
But spent it gay an' free on their betters – such as me –
  For the good advice I gave.

The men that fought at Minden, they was civil – yuss,
    they was –
  Never didn't talk o' rights an' wrongs,
But they got it with the toe (same as you will get it –
    so!) –
  For interrupting songs.

The men that fought at Minden, they was several other
    things
  Which I don't remember clear;
But *that's* the reason why, now the six-year men are dry,
  The rooks will stand the beer!

   Then do not be discouraged, 'Eaven is your 'elper,
    We'll learn you not to forget;
   An' you mustn't swear an' curse, or you'll only catch it
    worse,
    And we'll make you soldiers yet!

   Soldiers yet, if you've got it in you –
    All for the sake of the Core;
   Soldiers yet, if we 'ave to skin you –
    Run an' get the beer, Johnny Raw – Johnny Raw!
    Ho! run an' get the beer, Johnny Raw!

25 Bill 'Awkins

"As anybody seen Bill 'Awkins?"
  'Now 'ow in the devil would I know?'
"E's taken my girl out walkin'.
    An' I've got to tell 'im so—
      Gawd—bless—'im!
    I've got to tell 'im so.'

  'D'yer know what 'e's like. Bill 'Awkins?'
    'Now what in the devil would I care?'
"E's the livin', breathin' image of an organ-
      grinder's monkey,
    With a pound of grease in 'is 'air—
      Gawd—bless—'im!
    An' a pound o' grease in 'is air.'

  'An' s'pose you met Bill 'Awkins,
    Now what in the devil 'ud ye do?'
'I'd open 'is cheek to 'is chin-strap buckle,
    An' bung up 'is both eyes, too—
      Gawd—bless—'im!
    An' bung up 'is both eyes, too!'

  'Look 'ere, where 'e comes, Bill 'Awkins!
    Now what in the devil will you say?'
'It isn't fit an' proper to be fightin' on a Sunday,
    So I'll pass 'im the time o' day—
      Gawd—bless—'im!
    I'll pass 'im the time o' day!'

26 The Shut-Eye Sentry

Sez the Junior Orderly Sergeant
  To the Senior Orderly Man:
'Our Orderly Orf'cer's *hokee-mut*,
  You 'elp 'im all you can.
For the wine was old and the night is cold.
  An' the best we may go wrong,
So, 'fore 'e gits to the sentry-box,
  You pass the word along.'

So it was 'Rounds! What rounds?' at two of a frosty night,
  'E's 'oldin' on by the sergeant's sash, but, sentry, shut
    your eye.
An' it was 'Pass! All's well!' Oh, ain't 'e drippin' tight!
  'E'll need an affidavit pretty badly by-an'-by.

The moon was white on the barricks,
  The road was white an' wide,
An' the Orderly Orf'cer took it all,
  An' the ten-foot ditch beside.
An' the corporal pulled an' the sergeant pushed,
  An' the three they danced along,
But I'd shut my eyes in the sentry-box,
  So I didn't see nothin' wrong.

Though it was 'Rounds! What Rounds?' O corporal, 'old
  'im up!
'E's usin' 'is cap as it shouldn't be used, but, sentry,
    shut your eye.
An' it was 'Pass! All's well!' Ho, shun the foamin' cup!
  'E'll need, etc.

80

The Shut-Eye Sentry

'Twas after four in the mornin';
    We 'ad to stop the fun,
An' we sent 'im 'ome on a bullock-cart,
    With 'is belt an' stock undone;
But we sluiced 'im down an' we washed 'im out,
    An' a first-class job we made,
When we saved 'im, smart as a bombardier,
    For six o'clock parade.

It 'ad been 'Rounds! What Rounds?' Oh, shove 'im
    straight again!
  'E's usin' 'is sword for a bicycle, but, sentry, shut
    your eye.
An' it was 'Pass! All's well!' 'E's called me 'Darlin''
    Jane'!
  'E'll need, etc.

The drill was long an' 'eavy.
    The sky was 'ot an' blue.
An' 'is eye was wild an' 'is 'air was wet,
    But 'is sergeant pulled 'im through.
Our men was good old trusties –
    They'd done it on their 'ead;
But you ought to 'ave 'eard 'em markin' time
    To 'ide the things 'e said!

For it was 'Right flank – wheel!' for "Alt, an' stand at
    ease!'
  An' Left extend!' for 'Centre close!' O marker, shut
    your eye!
An' it was, "Ere, sir, 'ere! before the Colonel sees!'
  So he needed affidavits pretty badly by-an'-by.

There was two-an'-thirty sergeants,
    There was corp'rals forty-one,
There was just nine 'undred rank an' file
    To swear to a touch o' sun.
There was me 'e'd kissed in the sentry-box,
    As I 'ave not told in my song,
But I took my oath, which were Bible truth,
    I 'adn't seen nothin' wrong.

There's them that's 'ot an' 'aughty,
    There's them that's cold an' 'ard,
But there comes a night when the best gets tight,
    And then turns out the Guard.
I've seen them 'ide their liquor
    In every kind o' way,
But most depends on makin' friends
    With Privit Thomas A.!

When it is 'Rounds! What rounds?' 'E's breathin' through
    'is nose.
  'E's reelin', rollin', roarin' tight, but, sentry, shut
    your eye.
An' it is 'Pass! All's well!' An' that's the way it goes:
  We'll 'elp 'im for 'is mother, an' 'e'll 'elp us by-an'-by!

27 The Sergeant's Weddin'

'E was warned agin 'er —
    That's what made 'im look;
She was warned agin 'im —
    That is why she took.

The Sergeant's Weddin'

'Wouldn't 'ear no reason,
    'Went an' done it blind;
We know all about 'em,
    They've got all to find!

Cheer for the Sergeant's weddin' —
    Give 'em one cheer more!
Grey gun-'orses in the lando,
    An' a rogue is married to, etc.

What's the use o' tellin'
    'Arf the lot she's been?
'E's a bloomin' robber,
    An' 'e keeps canteen.
'Ow did 'e get 'is buggy?
    Gawd, you needn't ask!
'Made 'is forty gallon
    Out of every cask!

Watch 'im, with 'is 'air cut.
    Count us filin' by —
Won't the Colonel praise 'is
    Pop — u — lar — i — ty!
We 'ave scores to settle —
    Scores for more than beer;
She's the girl to pay 'em —
    That is why we're 'ere!

See the chaplain thinkin'?
    See the women smile?
Twig the married winkin'
    As they take the aisle?
Keep your side-arms quiet,
    Dressin' by the Band.
Ho! You 'oly beggars,
    Cough be'ind your 'and!

Now it's done an' over,
    'Ear the organ squeak,
"Voice that breathed o'er Eden' —
    Ain't she got the cheek!

White an' laylock ribbons,
    Think yourself so fine!
I'd pray Gawd to take yer
    'Fore I made yer mine.

Escort to the kerridge,
    Wish 'im luck, the brute!
Chuck the slippers after —
    [Pity 'taint a boot!]
Bowin' like a lady.
    Blushin' like a lad —
'Oo would say to see 'em
    Both is rotten bad?

Cheer for the Sergeant's weddin' —
    Give 'em one cheer more!
Grey gun-'orses in the lando,
    An' a rogue is married to; etc.

28 *The Mother-Lodge*

There was Rundle, Station Master,
    An' Beazeley of the Rail,
An' 'Ackman, Commissariat,
    An' Donkin' o' the Jail;
An' Blake, Conductor-Sargent,
    Our Master twice was 'e,
With 'im that kept the Europe-shop,
    Old Framjee Eduljee.

The Mother-Lodge

Outside — 'Sergeant! Sir! Salute! Salaam!'
Inside — 'Brother,' an' it doesn't do no 'arm.
We met upon the Level an' we parted on the Square,
An' I was Junior Deacon in my Mother Lodge out there!

We'd Bola Nath, Accountant,
  An' Saul the Aden Jew,
An' Din Mohammed, draughtsman
  Of the Survey Office too;
There was Babu Chuckerbutty,
  An' Amir Singh the Sikh,
An' Castro from the fittin'-sheds,
  The Roman Catholick!

We 'adn't good regalia,
  An' our Lodge was old an' bare,
But we knew the Ancient Landmarks,
  An' we kep' 'em to a hair;
An' lookin' on it backwards
  It often strikes me thus,
There ain't such things as infidels,
  Excep', per'aps, it's us.

For monthly, after Labour,
  We'd all sit down and smoke
(We dursn't give no banquits,
  Lest a Brother's caste were broke),
An' man on man got talkin'
  Religion an' the rest,
An' every man comparin'
  Of the God 'e knew the best.

So man on man got talkin',
    An' not a Brother stirred
Till mornin' waked the parrots
    An' that dam' brain-fever-bird.
We'd say 'twas 'ighly curious,
    An' we'd all ride 'ome to bed,
With Mo'ammed, God, an' Shiva
    Changin' pickets in our 'ead.

Full oft on Guv'ment service
    This rovin' foot 'ath pressed,
An' bore fraternal greetin's
    To the Lodges east an' west.
Accordin' as commanded
    From Kohat to Singapore,
But I wish that I might see them
    In my Mother Lodge once more.

I wish that I might see them,
    My Brethren black an' brown,
With the trichies smellin' pleasant
    An' the *hog-darn*[1] passin' down;
An' the old khansamah[2] snorin'
    On the bottle-khana[3] floor,
Like a Master in good standing
    With my Mother Lodge once more.

Outside — 'Sergeant! Sir! Salute! Salaam!'
Inside — 'Brother,' an' it doesn't do no 'arm.
We met upon the Level an' we parted on the Square,
An' I was Junior Deacon in my Mother Lodge out there!

---

[1] Cigar-lighter.   [2] Butler.   [3] Pantry.

29 Sappers

When the Waters were dried an' the Earth did appear
  ('It's all one,' says the Sapper),
The Lord He created the Engineer,
  Her Majesty's Royal Engineer,
  With the rank and pay of a Sapper!

When the Flood come along for an extra monsoon,
'Twas Noah constructed the first pontoon
  To the plans of Her Majesty's, etc.

But after fatigue in the wet an' the sun,
Old Noah got drunk, which he wouldn't ha' done
  If he'd trained with, etc.

When the Tower o' Babel had mixed up men's *bat*,
Some clever civilian was managing that,
  An' none of, etc.

When the Jews had a fight at the foot of a hill,
Young Joshua ordered the sun to stand still,
  For he was a Captain of Engineers, etc.

When the Children of Israel made bricks without straw,
They were learnin' the regular work of our Corps,
  The work of, etc.

For ever since then, if a war they would wage,
Behold us a-shinin' on history's page –
  First page for, etc.

We lay down their sidings an' help 'em entrain,
An' we sweep up their mess through the bloomin' campaign,
   In the style of, etc.

They send us in front with a fuse an' a mine
To blow up the gates that are rushed by the Line,
   But bent by, etc.

They send us behind with a pick an' a spade,
To dig for the guns of a bullock-brigade
   Which has asked for, etc.
We work under escort in trousers and shirt,
An' the heathen they plug us tail-up in the dirt,
   Annoying, etc.

We blast out the rock an' we shovel the mud,
We make 'em good roads an' – they roll down the *khud*.
   Reporting, etc.

We make 'em their bridges, their wells, an' their huts,
An' the telegraph-wire the enemy cuts,
   An' it's blamed on, etc.

An' when we return, an' from war we would cease,
They grudge us adornin' the billets of peace,
   Which are kept for, etc.

We build 'em nice barracks – they swear they are bad,
That our Colonels are Methodist, married or mad,
   Insultin', etc.

They haven't no manners nor gratitudes too,
For the more that we help 'em, the less will they do,
   But mock at, etc.

Now the Line's but a man with a gun in his hand,
An' Cavalry's only what horses can stand,
   When helped by, etc.

Artillery moves by the leave o' the ground,
But *we* are the men that do something all round,
   For *we* are, etc.

I have stated it plain, an' my argument's thus
   ('It's all one,' says the Sapper),
There's only one Corps which is perfect – that's us;
   An' they call us Her Majesty's Engineers,
   Her Majesty's Royal Engineers,
   With the rank and pay of a Sapper!

30 *'Soldier an' Sailor Too'*

As I was spittin' into the Ditch aboard o' the *Crocodile*,
I seed a man on a man-o'-war got up in the Reg'lars' style.
'E was scrapin' the paint from off of 'er plates, an' I sez to
   'im, "Oo are you?"
Sez 'e, 'I'm a Jolly – 'Er Majesty's Jolly – soldier an'
   sailor too!'
Now 'is work begins by Gawd knows when, and 'is work is
   never through;
'E isn't one o' the reg'lar Line, nor e' isn't one of the crew.
'E's a kind of a giddy harumfrodite – soldier an' sailor too!

An' after I met 'im all over the world, a doin' all kinds
   of things,
Like landin' 'isself with a Gatlin' gun to talk to them
   'eathen kings;

'E sleeps in an 'ammick instead of a cot, an' 'e drills with the
    deck on a slew,
An' 'e sweats like a Jolly — 'Er Majesty's Jolly — soldier an'
    sailor too!
For there isn't a job on the top o' the earth the beggar don't
    know, nor do —
You can leave 'im at night on a bald man's 'ead, to paddle
    'is own canoe —
'E's a sort of a bloomin' cosmopolouse — soldier an' sailor too.

We've fought 'em in trooper, we've fought 'em in dock, and
    drunk with 'em in betweens,
When they called us the seasick scull'ry-maids, an we called
    'em the Ass Marines;
But, when we was down for a double fatigue, from Wool-
    wich to Bernardmyo,
We sent for the Jollies — 'Er Majesty's Jollies — soldier an'
    sailor too!
They think for 'emselves, an' they steal for 'emselves, and
    they never ask what's to do,
But they're camped an' fed an' they're up an' fed before our
    bugle's blew.
Ho! they ain't no limpin' procrastitutes — soldier an' sailor too.

You may say we are fond of an 'arness-cut, or 'ootin' in
    barrick-yards,
Or startin' a Board School mutiny along o' the Onion
    Guards;
But once in a while we can finish in style for the ends of the
    earth to view,
The same as the Jollies — 'Er Majesty's Jollies — soldier an'
    sailor too!
They come of our lot, they was brothers to us; they was
    beggars we'd met an' knew;

'Soldier an' Sailor Too'

Yes, barrin' an inch in the chest an' the arm, they was
    doubles o' me an' you;
For they weren't no special chrysanthemums – soldier an'
    sailor too!

To take your chance in the thick of a rush, with firing
    all about,
Is nothing so bad when you've cover to 'and, an' leave an'
    likin' to shout;
But to stand an' be still to the *Birken'ead* drill is a damn
    tough bullet to chew,
An' they done it, the Jollies – 'Er Majesty's Jollies – soldier
    an' sailor too!
Their work was done when it 'adn't begun; they was younger
    nor me an' you;
Their choice it was plain between drownin' in 'eaps an' bein'
    mopped by the screw,
So they stood an' was still to the *Birken'ead* drill, soldier an'
    sailor too!

We're most of us liars, we're 'arf of us thieves, an' the rest
    are as rank as can be,
But once in a while we can finish in style (which I 'ope it
    won't 'appen to me).
But it makes you think better o' you an' your friends, an' the
    work you may 'ave to do,
When you think o' the sinkin' *Victorier's* Jollies – soldier an'
    sailor too!
Now there isn't no room for to say ye don't know – they 'ave
    proved it plain and true –
That whether it's Widow, or whether it's ship, Victorier's
    work is to do,
An' they done it, the Jollies – 'Er Majesty's Jollies – soldier
    an' sailor too!

31 'Bobs'

There's a little red-faced man,
  Which is Bobs,
Rides the tallest 'orse 'e can –
  Our Bobs.
If it bucks or kicks or rears,
'E can sit for twenty years
With a smile round both 'is ears –
  Can't yer, Bobs?
Then 'ere's to Bobs Bahadur – little Bobs,
    Bobs, Bobs!
'E's our pukka Kandaharder –
  Fightin' Bobs, Bobs, Bobs!
'E's the Dook of *Aggy Chel;*[1]
'E's the man that done us well,
An' we'll follow 'im to 'ell –
  Won't we, Bobs?

If a limber's slipped a trace,
  'Ook on Bobs.
If a marker's lost 'is place,
  Dress by Bobs.

For 'e's eyes all up 'is coat,
An' a bugle in 'is throat,
An' you will not play the goat
  Under Bobs.

'E's a little down on drink,
  Chaplain Bobs;
But it keeps us outer Clink –
  Don't it, Bobs?

  [1] Get ahead.

'Bobs'

So we will not complain
Tho' 'e's water on the brain,
If 'e leads us straight again –
   Blue-light[1] Bobs.

If you stood 'im on 'is head,
   Father Bobs,
You could spill a quart of lead
   Outer Bobs.
'E's been at it thirty years,
An' amassin' souveneers
In the way o' slugs an' spears –
   Ain't yer, Bobs?

What 'e does not know o' war,
   Gen'ral Bobs,
You can arst the shop next door –
   Can't they, Bobs?
Oh, 'e's little but he's wise,
'E's a terror for 'is size,
An' – 'e – *does* – *not* – *advertise* –
   Do yer, Bobs?

Now they've made a bloomin' Lord
   Outer Bobs,
Which was but 'is fair reward –
   Weren't it, Bobs?
So 'e'll wear a coronet
Where 'is 'elmet used to set;
But we know you won't forget –
   Will yer, Bobs?

Then 'ere's to Bobs Bahadur – little Bobs,
   Bobs, Bobs,

[1] Temperance.

93

Pocket-Wellin'ton an' *arder*[1] –
Fightin' Bobs, Bobs, Bobs!
This ain't no bloomin' ode,
But you've 'elped the soldier's load,
An' for benefits bestowed,
    Bless yer, Bobs!

32 *The Jacket*

Through the Plagues of Egyp' we was chasin' Arabi,
   Gettin' down an' shovin' in the sun;
An' you might 'ave called us dirty, an' you might ha' called
   us dry,
   An' you might 'ave 'eard us talkin' at the gun.
But the Captain 'ad 'is jacket, an' the jacket it was new –
   ('Orse Gunners, listen to my song!)
An' the wettin' of the jacket is the proper thing to do,
   Nor we didn't keep 'im waiting very long.

One day they gave us orders for to shell a sand redoubt,
   Loadin' down the axle-arms with case;
But the Captain knew 'is dooty, an' he took the crackers out
   An' he put some proper liquor in its place.
An' the Captain saw the shrapnel, which is six-an'-thirty
   clear.
   ('Orse Gunners, listen to my song!)
'Will you draw the weight,' sez 'e, 'or will you draw the
   beer?'
   An' we didn't keep 'im waitin' very long.
   For the Captain, etc.

[1] And a half.

The Jacket

Then we trotted gentle, not to break the bloomin' glass,
    Through the Arabites 'ad all their ranges marked;
But we dursn't 'ardly gallop, for the most was bottled Bass,
    An' we'd dreamed of it since we was disembarked:
So we fired economic with the shells we 'ad in 'and,
    ('Orse Gunners, listen to my song!)
But the beggars under cover 'ad the impidence to stand,
    An' we couldn't keep 'em waitin' very long.
       And the Captain, etc.

So we finished 'arf the liquor (an' the Captain took
    champagne),
    An' the Arabites was shootin' all the while;
An' we left our wounded 'appy with the empties on the plain,
    An' we used the bloomin' guns for pro-jectile!
We limbered up an' galloped – there were nothin' else to do –
    ('Orse Gunners, listen to my song!)
An' the Battery came a-boundin' like a boundin' kangaroo,
    But they didn't watch us comin' very long.
       As the Captain, etc.

We was goin' most extended – we was drivin' very fine,
    An' the Arabites were loosin' 'igh an' wide,
Till the Captain took the glassy with a rattlin' right incline,
    An' we dropped upon their 'eads the other side.
Then we give 'em quarter – such as 'adn't up and cut
    ('Orse Gunners, listen to my song!),
An' the Captain stood a limberful of fizzy – somethin'
    Brutt,
But we didn't leave it fizzing very long.
       For the Captain, etc.

We might ha' been court-martialled, but it all come out
    all right
    When they signalled us to join the main command.
There was every round expended, there was every
    gunner tight,
    An' the Captain waved a corkscrew in 'is 'and.
      But the Captain 'ad 'is jacket, etc.

33 That Day

It got beyond all orders an' it got beyond all 'ope;
    It got to shammin' wounded an' retirin' from the 'alt.
'Ole companies was lookin' for the nearest road to slope;
    It were just a bloomin' knock-out — an' our fault!

    Now there ain't no chorus 'ere to give,
    Nor there ain't no band to play;
    An' I wish I was dead 'fore I done what I did,
    Or seen what I seed that day!

We was sick o' bein' punished, an' we let 'em know it, too;
    An' a company-commander up an' 'it us with a sword,
An' some one shouted "Ook it!' an' it come to *sove-ki-poo*,
    An' we chucked our rifles from us — O my Gawd!

There was thirty dead an' wounded on the ground we
    wouldn't keep —
    No, there wasn't more than twenty when the front begun
    to go;
But, Christ! along the line o' flight they cut us up like sheep,
    An' that was all we gained by doin' so.

That Day

I 'eard the knives be'ind me, but I dursn't face my man,
    Nor I don't know where I went to, 'cause I didn't 'alt to
      see,
Till I 'eard a beggar squealin' out for quarter as 'e ran,
    An' I thought I knew the voice an' – it was me!

We was 'idin' under bedsteads more than 'arf a march away;
    We was lyin' up like rabbits all about the country side;
An' the major cursed 'is Maker 'cause 'e lived to see that day,
    An' the colonel broke 'is sword acrost, an' cried.

We was rotten 'fore we started – we was never disci*plined*;
    We made it out a favour if an order was obeyed;
Yes, every little drummer 'ad 'is rights an' wrongs to mind,
    So we had to pay for teachin' – an' we paid!

The papers 'id it 'andsome, but you know the Army knows:
    We was put to groomin' camels till the regiments withdrew,
An' they gave us each a medal for subduin' England's foes,
    An' I 'ope you like me song – because it's true!

      An' there ain't no chorus 'ere to give,
        Nor there ain't no band to play;
      But I wish I was dead 'fore I done what I did,
        Or seen what I seed that day!

34 Cholera Camp

We've got the cholerer in camp – it's worse than forty fights;
We're dyin' in the wilderness the same as Isrulites;
It's before us, an' be'ind us, an' we cannot get away,
An' the doctor's just reported we've ten more to-day!

> *Oh, strike your camp an' go, the bugle's callin',*
> *The Rains are fallin' –*
> *The dead are bushed an' stoned to keep 'em safe below;*
> *The Band's a-doin' all she knows to cheer us;*
> *The chaplain's gone and prayed to Gawd to 'ear us –*
> *To 'ear us –*
> *O Lord, for it's a killin' of us so!*

Since August, when it started, it's been stickin' to our tail,
Though they've 'ad us out by marches an' they've 'ad us
     back by rail;
But it runs as fast as troop-trains, and we can not get
     away;
An' the sick-list to the Colonel makes ten more to-day.

There ain't no fun in women nor there ain't no bite to drink;
It's much too wet for shootin', we can only march and think;
An' at evenin', down the *nullahs*, we can 'ear the jackals say,
'Get up, you rotten beggars, you've ten more to-day!'

'Twould make a monkey cough to see our way o' doin'
     things –
Lieutenants takin' companies an' captains takin' wings,
An' Lances actin' Sergeants – eight file to obey –
For we've lots o' quick promotion on ten deaths a day!

98

Cholera Camp

Our Colonel's white an' twitterly — 'e gets no sleep nor food,
But mucks about in 'orspital where nothing does no good.
'E sends us 'eaps o' comforts, all bought from 'is pay —
But there aren't much comfort 'andy on ten deaths a day.

Our Chaplain's got a banjo, an' a skinny mule 'e rides,
An' the stuff 'e says an' sings us, Lord, it makes us split
    our sides!
With 'is black coat-tails a-bobbin' to *Ta-ra-ra Boom-der-ay!*
'E's the proper kind o' *padre* for ten deaths day.

An' Father Victor 'elps 'im with our Roman Catholicks —
He knows an 'eap of Irish songs an' rummy conjurin' tricks;
An' the two they works together when it comes to play
    or pray;
So we keep the ball a-rollin' on ten deaths a day.

We've got the cholerer in camp — we've got it 'ot an' sweet;
It ain't no Christmas dinner, but it's 'elped an' we must eat.
We've gone beyond the funkin', 'cause we've found it
    doesn't pay,
An' we're rockin' round the Districk on ten deaths a day!

     Then strike your camp an' go, the Rains are fallin',
       The Bugle's callin'!
     The dead are bushed an' stoned to keep 'em safe below!
     An' them that do not like it they can lump it,
     An' them that can not stand it they can jump it;
     We've got to die somewhere — some way — some 'ow —
     We might as well begin to do it now!
     Then, Number One, let down the tent-pole slow,
     Knock out the pegs an' 'old the corners — so!
     Fold in the flies, furl up the ropes, an' stow!
     Oh, strike — oh, strike your camp an' go!
       (Gawd 'elp us!)

35 'Follow Me 'Ome'

There was no one like 'im, 'Orse or Foot,
    Nor any o' the Guns I knew:
An' because it was so, why, o' course 'e went an' died,
    Which is just what the best men do.

    So it's knock out your pipes an' follow me!
    An' it's finish up your swipes an' follow me!
    Oh, 'ark to the big drum callin',
    Follow me – follow me 'ome!

'Is mare she neighs the 'ole day long,
    She paws the 'ole night through,
An' she won't take 'er feed 'cause o' waitin' for 'is step,
    Which is just what a beast would do.

'Is girl she goes with a bombardier
    Before 'er month is through;
An' the banns are up in church, for she's got the beggar
      hooked,
    Which is just what a girl would do.

We fought 'bout a dog – last week it were –
    No more than a round or two;
But I strook 'im cruel 'ard, an' I wish I 'adn't now.
    Which is just what a man can't do.

'E was all that I 'ad in the way of a friend,
    An' I've 'ad to find one new;
But I'd give my pay an' stripe for to get the beggar back,
    Which it's just too late to do.

So it's knock out your pipes an' follow me!
An' it's finish off your swipes an' follow me!
  Oh, 'ark to the fifes a-crawlin'!
    Follow me — follow me 'ome!

Take 'im away! 'E's gone where the best men go.
Take 'im away! An' the gun-wheels turnin' slow.
Take 'im away! There's more from the place 'e come.
Take 'im away, with the limber an' the drum.

For it's 'Three round's blank' an' follow me,
An' it's 'Thirteen rank' an' follow me;
  Oh, passin' the love o' women.
    Follow me — follow me 'ome!

36 'My girl she give me the go onst'

My girl she give me the go onst,
  When I was a London lad,
An' I went on the drink for a fortnight,
  An' then I went to the bad.
The Queen she give me a shillin'
  To fight for 'er over the seas;
But Guv'ment built me a fever-trap,
  An' Injia give me disease.

  Chorus. Ho! don't you 'eed what a girl says,
      An' don't you go for the beer;
    But I was an ass when I was at grass,
      An' that is why I'm here.

I fired a shot at a Afghan,
  The beggar 'e fired again,
An' I lay on my bed with a 'ole in my 'ed,
  An' missed the next campaign!
I up with my gun at a Burman
  Who carried a bloomin' *dah*,
But the cartridge stuck and the bay'nit bruk,
  An' all I got was the scar.

    Chorus. Ho! don't you aim at a Afghan,
      When you stand on the sky-line clear;
    An' don't you go for a Burman
      If none o' your friends is near.

I served my time for a corp'ral,
  An' wetted my stripes with pop,
For I went on the bend with a intimate friend,
  An' finished the night in the 'shop'.
I served my time for a sergeant;
  The colonel 'e sez 'No!
The most you'll see is a full C.B.'
  An' . . . very next night 'twas so.

    Chorus. Ho! don't you go for a corp'ral
      Unless your 'ed is clear;
    But I was an ass when I was at grass,
      An' that is why I'm 'ere.

I've tasted the luck o' the army
  In barrack an' camp an' clink,
An' I lost my tip through the bloomin' trip
  Along o' the women an' drink.
I'm down at the heel o' my service,
  An' when I am laid on the shelf,
My very wust friend from beginning to end
  By the blood of a mouse was myself!

Chorus. Ho! don't you 'eed what a girl says,
 An' don't you go for the beer;
But I was an ass when I was at grass
 An' that is why I'm 'ere.

37 *The Ladies*

I've taken my fun where I've found it;
 I've rogued an' I've ranged in my time;
I've 'ad my pickin' o' sweet'earts,
 An' four o' the lot was prime.
One was an 'arf-caste widow,
 One was a woman at Prome,
One was the wife of a *jemadar-sais*,[1]
 An' one is a girl at 'ome.

Now I aren't no 'and with the ladies,
 For, takin' 'em all along,
You never can say till you've tried 'em,
 An' then you are like to be wrong.
There's times when you'll think that you mightn't,
 There's times when you'll know that you might;
But the things you will learn from the Yellow an' Brown,
 They'll 'elp you a lot with the White!

I was a young un at 'Oogli,
 Shy as a girl to begin;
Aggie de Castrer she made me,
 An' Aggie was clever as sin;
Older than me, but my first un —
 More like a mother she were —
Showed me the way to promotion an' pay,
 An' I learned about women from 'er!

[1] Head-groom.

Then I was ordered to Burma,
   Actin' in charge o' Bazar,
An' I got me a tiddy live 'eathen
   Through buyin' supplies off 'er pa.
Funny an' yellow an' faithful —
   Doll in a teacup she were,
But we lived on the square, like a true-married pair,
   An' I learned about women from 'er!

Then we was shifted to Neemuch
   (Or I might ha' been keepin' 'er now),
An' I took with a shiny she-devil,
   The wife of a nigger at Mhow;
'Taught me the gipsy-folks' *bolee*;[1]
   Kind o' volcano she were,
For she knifed me one night 'cause I wished she was white,
   And I learned about women from 'er!

Then I come 'ome in the trooper,
   'Long of a kid o' sixteen—
Girl from a convent at Meerut,
   The straightest I ever 'ave seen.
Love at first sight was 'er trouble.
   She didn't know what it were;
An' I wouldn't do such, 'cause I liked 'er too much,
   But — I learned about women from 'er!

I've taken my fun where I've found it,
   An' now I must pay for my fun,
For the more you 'ave known o' the others
   The less will you settle to one;
An' the end of it's sittin' and thinkin',
   An' dreamin' Hell-fires to see;
So be warned by my lot (which I know you will not),
   An' learn about women from me!

[1] Slang.

'Mary, pity Women!'

What did the Colonel's Lady think?
  Nobody never knew.
Somebody asked the Sergeant's wife,
  An' she told 'em true!
When you get to a man in the case,
  They're like as a row of pins—
For the Colonel's Lady an' Judy O'Grady
Are sisters under their skins!

38 'Mary, pity Women!'

You call yourself a man,
  For all you used to swear,
An' leave me, as you can,
  My certain shame to bear?
  I 'ear! You do not care —
You done the worst you know.
  I 'ate you, grinnin' there. . . .
Ah, Gawd, I love you so!

Nice while it lasted, an' now it is over —
Tear out your 'eart an' good-bye to your lover!
What's the use o' grievin', when the mother that bore you
(Mary, pity women!) knew it all before you?

  It aren't no false alarm,
    The finish to your fun;
  You — you 'ave brung the 'arm,
    An' I'm the ruined one:
    An' now you'll off an' run

With some new fool in tow.
    Your 'eart? You 'aven't none. . . .
Ah, Gawd, I love you so!

When a man is tired there is naught will bind 'im;
All 'e solemn promised 'e will shove be'ind 'im.
What's the good o' prayin' for The Wrath to strike 'im
(Mary, pity women!), when the rest are like 'im?

What 'ope for me or – it?
    What's left for us to do?
I've walked with men a bit,
    But this – but this is you.
    So 'elp me Christ, it's true!
Where can I 'ide or go?
    You coward through and through! . . .
Ah, Gawd, I love you so!

All the more you give 'em the less are they for givin' –
Love lies dead, an' you can not kiss 'im livin'.
Down the road 'e led you there is no returnin'
(Mary, pity women!), but you're late in learnin'!

You'd like to treat me fair?
    You can't, because we're pore?
We'd starve? What do I care!
    We might, but *this* is shore!
    I want the name – no more –
The name, an' lines to show,
    An' not to be an 'ore. . . .
Ah, Gawd, I love you so!

For To Admire

What's the good o' pleadin', when the mother that bore you
(Mary, pity women!) knew it all before you?
Sleep on 'is promises an' wake to your sorrow
(Mary, pity women!), for we sail to-morrow!

39 *For To Admire*

The Injian Ocean sets an' smiles
    So sof', so bright, so bloomin' blue;
There aren't a wave for miles an' miles
    Excep' the jiggle from the screw.
The ship is swep', the day is done,
    The bugle's gone for smoke and play;
An' black ag'in' the settin' sun
    The Lascar sings, '*Hum deckty hai!*'[1]

    For to admire an' for to see,
        For to be'old this world so wide –
    It never done no good to me,
        But I can't drop it if I tried!

I see the sergeants pitchin' quoits,
    I 'ear the women laugh an' talk,
I spy upon the quarter-deck
    The orficers an' lydies walk.
I thinks about the things that was,
    An' leans an' looks acrost the sea,
Till spite of all the crowded ship
    There's no one lef' alive but me.

[1] I'm looking out.

107

The things that was which I 'ave seen,
    In barrick, camp, an' action too,
I tells them over by myself,
    An' sometimes wonders if they're true;
For they was odd — most awful odd —
    But all the same now they are o'er,
There must be 'eaps o' plenty such,
    An' if I wait I'll see some more.

Oh, I 'ave come upon the books,
    An' frequent broke a barrick rule,
An' stood beside an' watched myself
    Be'avin' like a bloomin' fool.
I paid my price for findin' out,
    Nor never grutched the price I paid,
But sat in Clink without my boots,
    Admirin' 'ow the world was made.

Be'old a crowd upon the beam,
    An' 'umped above the sea appears
Old Aden, like a barrick-stove
    That no one's lit for years an' years!
I passed by that when I began,
    An' I go 'ome the road I came,
A time-expired soldier-man
    With six years' service to 'is name.

My girl she said, 'Oh, stay with me!'
    My mother 'eld me to 'er breast.
They've never written none, an' so
    They must 'ave gone with all the rest —
With all the rest which I 'ave seen
    An' found an' known an' met along.

For To Admire

I cannot say the things I feel,
   And so I sing my evenin' song:

     For to admire an' for to see,
      For to be'old this world so wide —
     It never done no good to me,
      But I can't drop it if I tried!

III Service Songs

(all but No. 40 from *The Five Nations*, 1903)

40 *The Absent-minded Beggar*

When you've shouted 'Rule Britannia,' when you've sung 'God
    save the Queen,'
  When you've finished killing Kruger with your mouth,
Will you kindly drop a shilling in my little tambourine
  For a gentleman in khaki ordered South?
He's an absent-minded beggar, and his weaknesses are great –
  But we and Paul must take him as we find him –
He is out on active service, wiping something off a slate –
  And he's left a lot of little things behind him!
Duke's son – cook's son – son of a hundred kings –
  (Fifty thousand horse and foot going to Table Bay!)
Each of 'em doing his country's work
  (and who's to look after their things?)
Pass the hat for your credit's sake,
               and pay – pay – pay!

There are girls he married secret, asking no permission to,
  For he knew he wouldn't get it if he did.

There is gas and coals and vittles, and the house-rent falling due,
    And it's more than rather likely there's a kid.
There are girls he walked with casual. They'll be sorry now
      he's gone,
    For an absent-minded beggar they will find him,
But it ain't the time for sermons with the winter coming on.
    We must help the girl that Tommy's left behind him!
Cook's son – Duke's son – son of a belted Earl –
    Son of a Lambeth publican – it's all the same to-day!
Each of 'em doing his country's work
    (and who's to look after the girl?)
Pass the hat for your credit's sake,
              and pay – pay – pay!

There are families by thousands, far too proud to beg or speak,
    And they'll put their sticks and bedding up the spout,
And they'll live on half o' nothing, paid 'em punctual once a week,
    'Cause the man that earns the wage is ordered out.
He's an absent-minded beggar, but he heard his country call,
    And his reg'ment didn't need to send to find him!
He chucked his job and joined it – so the job before us all
    Is to help the home that Tommy's left behind him!
Duke's job – cook's job – gardener, baronet, groom,
    Mews or palace or paper-shop, there's someone gone away!
Each of 'em doing his country's work
    (and who's to look after the room?)
Pass the hat for your credit's sake,
              and pay – pay – pay!

Let us manage so as, later, we can look him in the face,
    And tell him – what he'd very much prefer –
That, while he saved the Empire, his employer saved his place,
    And his mates (that's you and me) looked out for *her*.
He's an absent-minded beggar and he may forget it all,
    But we do not want his kiddies to remind him

'That we sent 'em to the workhouse while their daddy
    hammered Paul,
  So we'll help the homes that Tommy left behind him!
Cook's home – Duke's home – home of a millionaire,
    (Fifty thousand horse and foot going to Table Bay!)
Each of 'em doing his country's work
    (and what have you got to spare?)
Pass the hat for your credit's sake,
               and pay – pay – pay!

41 *Stellenbosh*

(COMPOSITE COLUMNS)

The General 'eard the firin' on the flank,
  An' 'e sent a mounted man to bring 'im back
The silly, pushin' person's name an' rank
  'Oo'd dared to answer Brother Boer's attack.
For there might 'ave been a serious engagement,
  An' 'e might 'ave wasted 'alf a dozen men;
So 'e ordered 'im to stop 'is operations round the kopjes,
  An' 'e told 'im off before the Staff at ten!

    And it all goes into the laundry,
    But it never comes out in the wash,
    'Ow we're sugared about by the old men
    ('Eavy-sterned amateur old men!)
    That 'amper an' 'inder an' scold men
    For fear o' Stellenbosh!

The General 'ad 'produced a great effect,'
  The General 'ad the country cleared – almost;

The General ''ad no reason to expect,'
  And the Boers 'ad us bloomin' well on toast!
For we might 'ave crossed the drift before the twilight,
  Instead o' sitting down an' takin' root;
But we was not allowed, so the Boojers scooped the crowd,
  To the last survivin' bandolier an' boot.

The General saw the farm'ouse in 'is rear,
  With its stoep so nicely shaded from the sun;
Sez 'e, 'I'll pitch my tabernacle 'ere,'
  An' 'e kept us muckin' round till 'e 'ad done.
For 'e might 'ave caught the confluent pneumonia
  From sleepin' in his gaiters in the dew;
So 'e took a book an' dozed while the other columns closed,
And De Wet's commando out an' trickled through!

The General saw the mountain-range ahead,
  With their 'elios showin' saucy on the 'eight,
So 'e 'eld us to the level ground instead,
  An' telegraphed the Boojers wouldn't fight.
For 'e might 'ave gone an' sprayed 'em with a pompom,
  Or 'e might 'ave slung a squadron out to see —
But 'e wasn't takin' chances in them 'igh an' 'ostile kranzes —
  He was markin' time to earn a K.C.B.

The General got 'is decorations thick
  (The men that backed 'is lies could not complain),
The Staff 'ad D.S.O.'s till we was sick,
  An' the soldier — 'ad the work to do again!
For 'e might 'ave known the District was a 'otbed,
  Instead of 'andin' over, upside-down,
To a man 'oo 'ad to fight 'alf a year to put it right,
  While the General went an' slandered 'im in town!

An' it all went into the laundry,
But it never came out in the wash.
We were sugared about by the old men
(Panicky, perishin' old men)
That 'amper an' 'inder an' scold men
For fear o' Stellenbosh!

42 Two Kopjes

(LESSON FOR YEOMANRY)

Only two African kopjes,
    Only the cart-tracks that wind
Empty and open between 'em,
    Only the Transvaal behind;
Only an Aldershot column
    Marching to conquer the land . . .
Only a sudden and solemn
    Visit, unarmed, to the Rand.

    Then scorn not the African kopje,
        The kopje that smiles in the heat,
    The wholly unoccupied kopje,
        The home of Cornelius and Piet.
    You can never be sure of your kopje,
        But of this be you blooming well sure,
    A kopje is always a kopje,
        And a Boojer is always a Boer!

Only two African kopjes,
    Only the vultures above,
Only baboons – at the bottom,
    Only some buck on the move;

Only a Kensington draper
   Only pretending to scout . . .
Only bad news for the paper,
   Only another knock-out.

      Then mock not the African kopje,
         And rub not your flank on its side,
      The silent and simmering kopje,
         The kopje beloved by the guide.
      You can never be, etc.

Only two African kopjes,
   Only the dust of their wheels,
Only a bolted commando,
   Only our guns at their heels . . .
Only a little barb-wire,
   Only a natural fort,
Only 'by sections retire,'
   Only 'regret to report'!

      Then mock not the African kopje,
         Especially when it is twins,
      One sharp and one table-topped kopje,
         For that's where the trouble begins.
      You never can be, etc.

Only two African kopjes
   Baited the same as before –
Only we've had it so often,
   Only we're taking no more . . .
Only a wave to our troopers,
   Only our flanks swinging past,
Only a dozen voorloopers,
   Only *we*'ve learned it at last!

Then mock not the African kopje,
    But take off your hat to the same,
The patient, impartial old kopje,
    The kopje that taught us the game!
For all that we knew in the Columns,
    And all they've forgot on the Staff,
We learned at the fight o' Two Kopjes,
    Which lasted two years an' a half.

O mock not the African kopje,
    Not even when peace has been signed —
The kopje that isn't a kopje —
    The kopje that copies its kind.
You can never be sure of your kopje,
    But of this be you blooming well sure,
That a kopje is always a kopje,
    And a Boojer is always a Boer!

43 *The Instructor*

(CORPORALS)

At times when under cover I 'ave said,
To keep my spirits up an' raise a laugh,
'Earin' 'im pass so busy over-'ead —
Old Nickel Neck, 'oo isn't on the Staff —
'*There's one above is greater than us all.*'

Before 'im I 'ave seen my Colonel fall,
An' watched 'im write my Captain's epitaph,
So that a long way off it could be read —
He '*as* the knack o' makin' men feel small —
Old Whistle Tip, 'oo isn't on the Staff.

117

There is no sense in fleein' (I 'ave fled),
Better go on an' do the belly-crawl,
An' 'ope 'e'll 'it some other man instead
Of you 'e seems to 'unt so speshual –
Fitzy van Spitz, 'oo isn't on the Staff.

An' thus in mem'ry's gratis biograph,
Now that the show is over, I recall
The peevish voice an' 'oary mushroom 'ead
Of 'im we owned was greater than us all,
'Oo give instruction to the quick an' the dead –
The Shudderin' Beggar not upon the Staff.

44 *Boots*

(INFANTRY COLUMNS OF THE EARLIER WAR)

We're foot – slog – slog – slog – sloggin' over Africa!
Foot – foot – foot – foot – sloggin' over Africa –
(Boots – boots – boots – boots, movin' up and down again!)
There's no discharge in the war!

Seven – six – eleven – five – nine-an'-twenty mile to-day –
Four – eleven – seventeen – thirty-two the day before –
(Boots – boots – boots – boots, movin' up and down again!)
There's no discharge in the war!

Don't – don't – don't – don't – look at what's in front of you
(Boots – boots – boots – boots, movin' up an' down again);
Men – men – men – men – men go mad with watchin' 'em,
An' there's no discharge in the war.

Boots

Try — try — try — try — to think o' something different —
Oh — my — God — keep — me from goin' lunatic!
(Boots — boots — boots — boots, movin' up an' down again!)
    There's no discharge in the war

Count — count — count — count — the bullets in the bandoliers;
If — your — eyes — drop — they will get atop o' you
(Boots — boots — boots — boots, movin' up and down again) —
    There's no discharge in the war!

We — can — stick — out — 'unger, thirst, an' weariness,
But — not — not — not — not the chronic sight of 'em —
Boots — boots — boots — boots, movin' up an' down again,
    An' there's no discharge in the war!

'Tain't — so — bad — by — day because o' company,
But night — brings — long — strings o' forty thousand million
Boots — boots — boots — boots, movin' up an' down again.
    There's no discharge in the war!

I — 'ave — marched — six — weeks in 'Ell an' certify
It — is — not — fire — devils dark or anything
But boots — boots — boots, movin' up an' down again.
    An' there's no discharge in the war!

45 *The Married Man*

(RESERVIST OF THE LINE)

The bachelor 'e fights for one
    As joyful as can be;
But the married man don't call it fun,
    Because 'e fights for three —
For 'Im an' 'Er an' It
    (An' Two an' One makes Three)
'E wants to finish 'is little bit,
    An' 'e wants to go 'ome to 'is tea!

The bachelor pokes up 'is 'ead
    To see if you are gone;
But the married man lies down instead,
    An' waits till the sights come on.
For 'Im an' 'Er an' a hit
    (Direct or ricochee)
'E wants to finish 'is little bit,
    An' 'e wants to go 'ome to 'is tea.

The bachelor will miss you clear
    To fight another day;
But the married man, 'e says 'No fear!'
    'E wants you out of the way
Of 'Im an' 'Er an' It
    (An' 'is road to 'is farm or the sea),
'E wants to finish 'is little bit,
    An' 'e wants to go 'ome to 'is tea.

The bachelor 'e fights 'is fight
    An' stretches out an' snores;

The Married Man

But the married man sits up all night –
    For 'e don't like out o' doors:
'E'll strain an' listen an' peer
    An' give the first alarm –
For the sake o' the breathin' 'e's used to 'ear
    An' the 'ead on the thick of 'is arm.

The bachelor may risk 'is 'ide
    To 'elp you when you're downed;
But the married man will wait beside
    Till the ambulance comes round.
'E'll take your 'ome address
    An' all you've time to say,
Or if 'e sees there's 'ope, 'e'll press
    Your art'ry 'alf the day –

For 'Im an' 'Er an' It
    (An' One from Three leaves Two),
For 'e knows you wanted to finish your bit,
    An' 'e knows 'oo's wantin' you.
Yes, 'Im an' 'Er an' It
    (Our 'oly One in Three),
We're all of us anxious to finish our bit,
    An' we want to get 'ome to our tea!

Yes, It an' 'Er an' 'Im,
    Which often makes me think
The married man must sink or swim
    An' – 'e can't afford to sink!
Oh 'Im an' It an' 'Er
    Since Adam an' Eve began,
So I'd rather fight with the bacheler
    An' be nursed by the married man!

46 Ubique

(ROYAL ARTILLERY)

There is a word you often see, pronounce it as you may –
'You bike,' 'you bykwe,' 'ubbikwe' – alludin' to R.A.
It serves 'Orse, Field, an' Garrison as motto for a crest,
An' when you've found out all it means I'll tell you 'alf the rest.

Ubique means the long-range Krupp be'ind the low-range 'ill –
Ubique means you'll pick it up an' while you do stand still.
Ubique means you've caught the flash an' timed it by the sound.
Ubique means five gunners' 'ash before you've loosed a round.

Ubique means Blue Fuse, an' make the 'ole to sink the trail.
Ubique means stand up an' take the Mauser's 'alf-mile 'ail.
Ubique means the crazy team not God nor man can 'old.
Ubique means that 'orse's scream which turns your innards cold!

Ubique means 'Bank, 'Olborn, Bank – a penny all the way' –
The soothin', jingle-bump-an'-clank from day to peaceful day.
Ubique means 'They've caught De Wet, an' now we shan't
            be long.'
Ubique means 'I much regret, the beggar's goin' strong!'

Ubique means the tearin' drift where, breech-blocks jammed
            with mud,
The khaki muzzles duck an' lift across the khaki flood.
Ubique means the dancing plain that changes rocks to Boers.
Ubique means mirage again an' shellin' all outdoors.

Ubique means 'Entrain at once for Grootdefeatfontein'!
Ubique means 'Off-load your guns' – at midnight in the rain!
Ubique means 'More mounted men. Return all guns to store.'
Ubique means the R.A.M.R. Infantillery Corps!

Columns

Ubique means that warnin' grunt the perished linesman knows,
When o'er 'is strung an' sufferin' front the shrapnel sprays
    'is foes;
An' as their firin' dies away the 'usky whisper runs
From lips that 'aven't drunk all day: 'The Guns, Thank Gawd,
    the Guns!'

Extreme, depressed, point-blank or short, end-first or any'ow,
From Colesberg Kop to Quagga's Poort – from Ninety-Nine
    till now –
By what I've 'eard the others tell an' I in spots 'ave seen,
There's nothin' this side 'Eaven or 'Ell Ubique doesn't mean!

47 *Columns*

(MOBILE COLUMNS OF THE LATER WAR)

Out o' the wilderness, dusty an' dry
    (*Time, an' 'igh time to be trekkin' again!*)
'Oo is it 'eads to the Detail Supply?
    (*A section, a pompom, an' six 'undred men*).

'Ere comes the clerk with 'is lantern an' keys
    (*Time, an' 'igh time to be trekkin' again!*)
'Surplus of everything – draw what you please
    '*For the section, the pompom, an' six 'undred men.*'

'What are our orders an' where do we lay?'
    (*Time, an' igh time to be trekkin' again!*)
'You came after dark – you will leave before day,
    '*You section, you pompom, an' six 'undred men!*'

Down the tin street, 'alf awake an' unfed,
'Ark to 'em blessin' the Gen'ral in bed!
Now by the church an' the outspan they wind –
Over the ridge an' it's all lef' be'ind
    For the section, etc.

Soon they will camp as the dawn's growin' grey,
Roll up for coffee an' sleep while they may –
    The section, etc.

Read their 'ome letters, their papers an' such,
For they'll move after dark to astonish the Dutch
    With a section, etc.

'Untin' for shade as the long hours pass,
Blankets on rifles or burrows in grass,
    Lies the section, etc.

Dossin' or beatin' a shirt in the sun,
Watching chameleons or cleanin' a gun,
    Waits the section, etc.

With nothin' but stillness as far as you please,
An' the silly mirage stringin' islands an' seas
    Round the section, etc.

So they strips off their hide an' they grills in their bones,
Till the shadows crawl out from beneath the pore stones
    Towards the section, etc.

An' the Mauser-bird stops an' the jackals begin,
An' the 'orse-guard comes up and the Gunners 'ook in
    As a 'int to the pompom an' six 'undred men. . . . .

Columns

Off through the dark with the stars to rely on –
(Alpha Centauri an' somethin 'Orion)
Moves the section, etc.

Same bloomin' 'ole which the ant-bear 'as broke,
Same bloomin' stumble an' same bloomin' joke
Down the section, etc.

Same 'which is right?' where the cart-tracks divide,
Same 'give it up' from the same clever guide
To the section, etc.

Same tumble-down on the same 'idden farm,
Same white-eyed Kaffir 'oo gives the alarm
Of the section, etc.

Same shootin' wild at the end o' the night,
Same flyin' tackle an' same messy fight
By the section, etc.

Same ugly 'iccup an' same 'orrid squeal,
When it's too dark to see an' it's too late to feel
In the section, etc.

(Same batch of prisoners, 'airy an' still,
Watchin' their comrades bolt over the 'ill
From the section, etc.)

Same chilly glare in the eye of the sun
As 'e gets up displeasured to see what was done
By the section, etc.

Same splash o' pink on the stoep or the kraal,
An' the same quiet face which 'as finished with all
In the section, the pompom, an' six 'undred men.

Out o' the wilderness, dusty an' dry
    (*Time, an' 'igh time to be trekkin' again!*)
'Oo is it 'eads to the Detail Supply?
    (*A section, a pompom, an' six 'undred men*).

48 M. I.

(MOUNTED INFANTRY OF THE LINE)

I wish my mother could see me now, with a fence-post under
    my arm,
And a knife and a spoon in my putties that I found on a Boer farm,
Atop of a sore-backed Argentine, with a thirst that you
    couldn't buy.
    I used to be in the Yorkshires once
    (Sussex, Lincolns, and Rifles once),
    Hampshires, Glosters, and Scottish once! (*ad lib*)
        But now I am M. I.

That is what we are known as — that is the name you must call
If you want officers' servants, pickets an' 'orseguards an' all —
Details for buryin'-parties, company-cooks or supply —
Turn out the chronic Ikonas! Roll up the ——[1] M. I.!

My 'ands are spotty with veldt-sores, my shirt is a button
    an' frill,
An' the things I've used my bay'nit for would make a tinker ill!
An' I don't know whose dam' column I'm in, nor where we're
    trekkin' nor why.

[1] Number according to taste and service of audience.

126

M. I.

I've trekked from the Vaal to the Orange once –
From the Vaal to the greasy Pongolo once –
(Or else it was called the Zambesi once) –
                    For now I am M. I.

That is what we are known as – we are the push you require
For outposts all night under freezin', an' rearguard all day
        under fire.
Anything 'ot or unwholesome? Anything dusty or dry?
Borrow a bunch of Ikonas! Trot out the —— M. I.!

Our Sergeant-Major's a subaltern, our Captain's a Fusilier –
Our Adjutant's 'late of Somebody's 'Orse,' an' a Melbourne
        auctioneer;
But you couldn't spot us at 'arf a mile from the crackest caval-ry.
        They used to talk about Lancers once,
        Hussars, Dragoons, an' Lancers once,
        'Elmets, pistols, an' carbines once,
                    But now we are M. I.

That is what we are known as – we are the orphans they blame
For beggin' the loan of an 'ead-stall an' makin' a mount to the same:
Can't even look at an 'orselines but some one goes bellerin' 'Hi!
'Ere comes a burglin' Ikona!' Footsack you —— M. I.!

We're trekkin' our twenty miles a day an' bein' loved by the Dutch,
But we don't hold on by the mane no more, nor lose our stirrups –
        much;
An' we scout with a senior man in charge where the 'oly white
        flags fly.
        We used to think they were friendly once,
        Didn't take any precautions once
        (Once, my ducky, an' only once!)
                    But now we are M. I.

127

That is what we are known as – we are the beggars that got
Three days 'to learn equitation,' an' six months o' bloomin' well
    trot!
Cow-guns, an' cattle, an' convoys – an' Mister De Wet on the fly –
We are the rollin' Ikonas! We are the —— M. I.!

The new fat regiments come from home, imaginin' vain V.C.'s
(The same as our talky-fighty men which are often Number
    Threes[1]),
But our words o' command are 'Scatter' an' 'Close' an' 'Let your
    wounded lie.'
  We used to rescue 'em noble once, –
  Givin' the range as we raised 'em once,
  Gettin' 'em killed as we saved 'em once –
          But now we are M. I.

That is what we are known as – we are the lanterns you view
After a fight round the kopjes, lookin' for men that we knew;
Whistlin' an' callin' together, 'altin' to catch the reply: –
"Elp me! O 'elp me, Ikonas!' This way, the —— M. I.!

I wish my mother could see me now, a-gatherin' news on my own,
When I ride like a General up to the scrub and ride back like
    Tod Sloan,
Remarkable close to my 'orse's neck to let the shots go by.
  We used to fancy it risky once
  (Called it a reconnaissance once),
  Under the charge of an orf'cer once,
          But now we are M. I.

That is what we are known as – that is the song you must say
When you want men to be Mausered at one and a penny a day;
We are no five-bob colonials – we are the 'ome-made supply,
Ask for the London Ikonas! Ring up the —— M. I.!

[1] Horse-holders when in action, and therefore generally under cover.

M. I.

I wish myself could talk to myself as I left 'im a year ago;
I could tell 'im a lot that would save 'im a lot on the things that 'e
    ought to know!
When I think o' that ignorant barrack-bird, it almost makes
    me cry.
  I used to belong in an Army once
  (Gawd! what a rum little Army once)
  Red little, dead little Army once!
           But now I am M. I.!

That is what we are known as — we are the men that have been
Over a year at the business, smelt it an' felt it an' seen.
We 'ave got 'old of the needful — *you* will be told by and by;
Wait till you've 'eard the Ikonas, spoke to the old M. I.!

Mount — march, Ikonas! Stand to your 'orses again!
Mop off the frost on the saddles, mop up the miles on the plain.
Out go the stars in the dawnin', up goes our dust to the sky,
Walk — trot, Ikonas! Trek jou,[1] *the old M. I.!*

49 Lichtenberg

(N.S.W. CONTINGENT)

  Smells are surer than sounds or sights
    To make your heart-strings crack —
  They start those awful voices o' nights
    That whisper, 'Old man, come back.'
  That must be why the big things pass
    And the little things remain,
  Like the smell of the wattle by Lichtenberg,
    Riding in, in the rain.

[1] Get ahead.

There was some silly fire on the flank
   And the small wet drizzling down –
There were the sold-out shops and the bank
   And the wet, wide-open town;
And we were doing escort-duty
   To somebody's baggage-train,
And I smelt wattle by Lichtenberg –
   Riding in, in the rain.

It was all Australia to me –
   All I had found or missed:
Every face I was crazy to see,
   And every woman I'd kissed:
All that I shouldn't ha' done, God knows!
   (As He knows I'll do it again),
That smell of the wattle round Lichtenberg,
   Riding in, in the rain!

And I saw Sydney the same as ever,
   The picnics and brass-bands;
And the little homestead on Hunter River
   And my new vines joining hands.
It all came over me in one act
   Quick as a shot through the brain –
With the smell of the wattle round Lichtenberg,
   Riding in, in the rain.

I have forgotten a hundred fights,
   But one I shall not forget –
With the raindrops bunging up my sights
   And my eyes bunged up with wet:
And through the crack and the stink of the cordite
   (Ah Christ! My country again!)
The smell of the wattle by Lichtenberg,
   Riding in, in the rain!

50 *The Parting of the Columns*

'. . . On the –th instant a mixed detachment of colonials left
—— for Cape Town, there to rejoin their respective homeward-
bound contingents, after fifteen months' service in the field.
They were escorted to the station by the regular troops in garrison and the bulk of Colonel ——'s column, which has just come
in to refit, preparatory to further operations. The leave-taking
was of the most cordial character, the men cheering each other
continuously.'—*Any Newspaper.*

We've rode and fought and ate and drunk as rations come to hand,
Together for a year and more around this stinkin' land:
Now you are goin' home again, but we must see it through.
We needn't tell we liked you well. Good-bye – good luck to you!

You 'ad no special call to come, and so you doubled out,
And learned us how to camp and cook an' steal a horse and scout:
Whatever game we fancied most, you joyful played it too,
And rather better on the whole. Good-bye – good luck to you!

There isn't much we 'aven't shared, since Kruger cut and run,
The same old work, the same old skoff, the same old dust and sun;
The same old chance that laid us out, or winked an' let us through;
The same old Life, the same old Death. Good-bye – good luck
    to you!

Our blood 'as truly mixed with yours – all down the Red Cross
    train,
We've bit the same thermometer in Bloeming-typhoidtein.
We've 'ad the same old temp'rature – the same relapses too,
The same old saw-backed fever-chart. Good-bye – good luck
    to you!

But 'twasn't merely this an' that (which all the world may know),
'Twas how you talked an' looked at things which made us like
   you so.
All independent, queer an' odd, but most amazin' new,
My word! you shook us up to rights. Good-bye – good luck to you!

Think o' the stories round the fire, the tales along the trek –
O' Calgary an' Wellin'ton, an' Sydney and Quebec;
Of mine an' farm, an' ranch an' run, an' moose an' cariboo,
An' parrots peckin' lambs to death! Good-bye – good luck to you!

We've seen you 'ome by word o' mouth, we've watched your rivers
   shine,
We've 'eard your bloomin' forests blow of eucalip' and pine:
Your young, gay countries north an' south, we feel we own
   'em too,
For they was made by rank an' file. Good-bye – good luck to you!

We'll never read the papers now without inquirin' first
For word from all those friendly dorps where you was born an'
   nursed.
Why, Dawson, Galle, an' Montreal – Port Darwin – Timaru,
They're only just across the road! Good-bye – good luck to you!

Good-bye! – So-long! Don't lose yourselves – nor us, nor all kind
   friends,
But tell the girls your side the drift we're comin' – when it ends!
Good-bye, you bloomin' Atlases! You've taught us somethin' new:
The world's no bigger than a kraal. Good-bye – good luck to you!

51 Half-Ballad of Waterval

When by the labour of my 'ands
  I've 'elped to pack a transport tight
With prisoners for foreign lands
  I ain't transported with delight.
  I know it's only just an' right,
    But yet it somehow sickens me,
For I 'ave learned at Waterval
    The meanin' of captivity.

Be'ind the pegged barb-wire strands,
  Beneath the tall electric light,
We used to walk in bare-'ead bands,
  Explainin' 'ow we lost our fight.
  An' that is what they'll do to-night
    Upon the steamer out at sea,
If I 'ave learned at Waterval
    The meanin' of captivity.

They'll never know the shame that brands –
  Black shame no livin' down makes white,
The mockin' from the sentry-stands,
  The women's laugh, the gaoler's spite.
  We are too bloomin' much polite,
    But that is 'ow I'd 'ave us be . . .
Since I 'ave learned at Waterval
    The meanin' of captivity.

133

They'll get those draggin' days all right,
  Spent as a foreigner commands,
An' 'orrors of the locked-up night,
  With 'Ell's own thinkin' on their 'ands.
  I'd give the gold o' twenty Rands
    (If it was mine) to set 'em free . . .
For I 'ave learned at Waterval
  The meanin' of captivity!

52 *Bridge-Guard in the Karroo*

'and will supply details to guard the Blood River Bridge.'
                      District Orders—Lines of Communication.

Sudden the desert changes,
  The raw glare softens and clings,
Till the aching Oudtshoorn ranges
  Stand up like the thrones of kings –

Ramparts of slaughter and peril –
  Blazing, amazing – aglow
'Twixt the sky-line's belting beryl
  And the wine-dark flats below.

Royal the pageant closes,
  Lit by the last of the sun –
Opal and ash-of-roses,
  Cinnamon, umber, and dun.

The twilight swallows the thicket,
  The starlight reveals the ridge;
The whistle shrills to the picket –
  We are changing guard on the bridge.

Bridge-Guard in the Karroo

(Few, forgotten and lonely,
  Where the empty metals shine —
No, not combatants — only
  Details guarding the line.)

We slip through the broken panel
  Of fence by the ganger's shed;
We drop to the waterless channel
  And the lean track overhead;

We stumble on refuse of rations,
  The beef and the biscuit-tins;
We take our appointed stations,
  And the endless night begins.

We hear the Hottentot herders
  As the sheep click past to the fold —
And the click of the restless girders
  As the steel contracts in the cold —

Voices of jackals calling
  And, loud in the hush between,
A morsel of dry earth falling
  From the flanks of the scarred ravine.

And the solemn firmament marches,
  And the hosts of heaven rise
Framed through the iron arches —
  Banded and barred by the ties,

Till we feel the far track humming,
  And we see her headlight plain,
And we gather and wait her coming —
  The wonderful north-bound train.

(Few, forgotten and lonely,
  Where the white car-windows shine –
No, not combatants – only
  Details guarding the line.)

Quick, ere the gift escape us!
  Out of the darkness we reach
For a handful of week-old papers
  And a mouthful of human speech.

And the monstrous heaven rejoices,
  And the earth allows again,
Meetings, greetings, and voices
  Of women talking with men.

So we return to our places,
  As out on the bridge she rolls;
And the darkness covers our faces,
  And the darkness re-enters our souls.

More than a little lonely
  Where the lessening tail-lights shine.
No – not combatants – only
  Details guarding the line!

53 'Wilful-Missing'

There is a world outside the one you know,
    To which for curiousness 'Ell can't compare –
It is the place where 'wilful-missings' go,
    As we can testify, for we are there.

You may 'ave read a bullet laid us low,
    That we was gathered in 'with reverent care'
And buried proper. But it was not so,
    As we can testify, for we are there.

They can't be certain – faces alter so
    After the old aasvogel's 'ad 'is share;
The uniform's the mark by which they go –
    And – ain't it odd? – the one we best can spare.

We might 'ave seen our chance to cut the show –
    Name, number, record, an' begin elsewhere –
Leavin' some not too late-lamented foe
    One funeral – private – British – for 'is share.

We may 'ave took it yonder in the Low
    Bush-veldt that sends men stragglin' unaware
Among the Kaffirs, till their columns go,
    An' they are left past call or count or care.

We might 'ave been your lovers long ago,
    'Usbands or children – comfort or despair.
Our death (an' burial) settles all we owe,
    An' why we done it is our own affair.

Marry again, and we will not say no,
    Nor come to bastardise the kids you bear,
Wait on in 'ope – you've all your life below,
    Before you'll ever 'ear us on the stair.

There is no need to give our reasons, though
    Gawd knows we all 'ad reasons which were fair;
But other people might not judge 'em so,
    And now it doesn't matter what they were.

What man can size or weigh another's woe?
    There are some things too bitter 'ard to bear.
Suffice it we 'ave finished — Domino!
    As we can testify, for we are there,
In the side-world where 'wilful-missings' go.

54 *Piet*

(REGULAR OF THE LINE)

I do not love my Empire's foes,
    Not call 'em angels; still,
What *is* the sense of 'atin' those
    'Oom you are paid to kill?
So, barrin' all that foreign lot
    Which only joined for spite,
Myself, I'd just as soon as not
    Respect the man I fight.
        Ah there, Piet! — 'is trousies to 'is knees,
        'Is coat-tails lyin' level in the bullet-sprinkled breeze;
        'E does not lose 'is rifle an' 'e does not lose 'is seat,
        I've known a lot o' people ride a dam' sight worse than Piet!

I've 'eard 'im cryin' from the ground
    Like Abel's blood of old,
An' skirmished out to look, an' found
    The beggar nearly cold;

Piet

I've waited on till 'e was dead
 (Which couldn't 'elp 'im much),
But many grateful things 'e's said
 To me for doin' such.
  Ah there, Piet! whose time 'as come to die,
  'Is carcase past rebellion, but 'is eyes inquirin' why.
  Though dressed in stolen uniform with badge o' rank complete,
  I've known a lot of fellers go a dam' sight worse than Piet.

An' when there wasn't aught to do
 But camp and cattle-guards,
I've fought with 'im the 'ole day through
 At fifteen 'undred yards;
Long afternoons o' lyin' still,
 An' 'earin' as you lay
The bullets swish from 'ill to 'ill
 Like scythes among the 'ay.
  Ah there, Piet! – be'ind 'is stony kop,
  With 'is Boer bread an' biltong, an' 'is flask of awful Dop;
  'Is Mauser for amusement an' 'is pony for retreat,
  I've known a lot o' fellers shoot a dam' sight worse than Piet.

He's shoved 'is rifle 'neath my nose
 Before I'd time to think,
An' borrowed all my Sunday clo'es
 An' sent me 'ome in pink;
An' I 'ave crept (Lord, 'ow I've crept!)
 On 'ands an' knees I've gone,
And spoored and floored and caught and kept
 An' sent him to Ceylon!
  Ah there, Piet! – you've sold me many a pup,
  When week on week alternate it was you an' me "ands up!"
  But though I never made *you* walk man-naked in the 'eat,
  I've know a lot of fellows stalk a dam' sight worse than Piet.

From Plewman's to Marabastad,
    From Ookiep to De Aar,
Me an' my trusty friend 'ave 'ad,
    As you might say, a war;
But seein' what both parties done
    Before 'e owned defeat,
I ain't more proud of 'avin' won.
    Than I am pleased with Piet.
        Ah there, Piet! – picked up be'ind the drive!
        The wonder wasn't 'ow 'e fought, but 'ow 'e kep' alive,
        With nothin' in 'is belly, on 'is back, or to 'is feet –
        I've known a lot 'o men behave a dam' sight worse than Piet.

No more I'll 'ear 'is rifle crack
    Along the block'ouse fence –
The beggar's on the peaceful tack,
    Regardless of expense.
For countin' what 'e eats an' draws,
    An' gifts an' loans as well,
'E's gettin' 'alf the Earth, because
    'E didn't give us 'Ell!
Ah there, Piet! with your brand-new English plough,
Your gratis tents an' cattle, an' your most ungrateful frow.
You've made the British taxpayer rebuild your country-seat –
I've known some pet battalions charge a dam' sight less than Piet.

55 Chant-Pagan

ENGLISH IRREGULAR: '99–02

Me that 'ave been what I've been,
Me that 'ave gone where I've gone,
Me that 'ave seen what I've seen –
    'Ow can I ever take on

Chant-Pagan

With awful old England again,
An' 'ouses both sides of the street,
And 'edges two sides of the lane,
And the parson an' 'gentry' between,
An' touchin' my 'at when we meet –
  Me that 'ave been what I've been?

Me that 'ave watched 'arf a world
'Eave up all shiny with dew,
Kopje on kop to the sun,
An' as soon as the mist let 'em through
Our 'elios winkin' like fun –
Three sides of a ninety-mile square,
Over valleys as big as a shire –
Are ye there? Are ye there? Are ye there?
An' then the blind drum of our fire . . .
An' I'm rollin' 'is lawns for the Squire,
              Me!

Me that 'ave rode through the dark
Forty mile often on end,
Along the Ma'ollisberg Range,
With only the stars for my mark
An' only the night for my friend,
An' things runnin' off as you pass,
An' things jumpin' up in the grass,
An' the silence, the shine an' the size
Of the 'igh, inexpressible skies. . . .
I am takin' some letters almost
As much as a mile, to the post,
An' 'mind you come back with the change!'
              Me!

Me that saw Barberton took
When we dropped through the clouds on their 'ead,
An' they 'ove the guns over and fled –
Me that was through Di'mond 'Ill,
An' Pieters an' Springs an' Belfast –
From Dundee to Vereeniging all!
Me that stuck out to the last
(An' five bloomin' bars on my chest) –
I am doin' my Sunday-school best,
By the 'elp of the Squire an' 'is wife
(Not to mention the 'ousemaid an' cook),
To come in an' 'ands up an' be still,
An' honestly work for my bread,
My livin' in that state of life
To which it shall please God to call
               Me!

Me that 'ave followed my trade
In the place where the lightnin's are made,
'Twixt the Rains and the Sun and the Moon;
Me that lay down an' got up
Three years an' the sky for my roof –
That 'ave ridden my 'unger an' thirst
Six thousand raw mile on the hoof,
With the Vaal and the Orange for cup,
An' the Brandwater Basin for dish, –
Oh! it's 'ard to be'ave as they wish,
(Too 'ard, an' a little too soon),
I'll 'ave to think over it first –
               Me!

I will arise an' get 'ence; –
I will trek South and make sure
If it's only my fancy or not
That the sunshine of England is pale.

And the breezes of England are stale,
An' there's somethin' gone small with the lot;
For *I* know of a sun an' a wind,
An' some plains and a mountain be'ind,
An' some graves by a barb-wire fence;
An' a Dutchman I've fought 'oo might give
Me a job were I ever inclined,
To look in an' offsaddle an' live
Where there's neither a road nor a tree –
But only my Maker an' me,
And I think it will kill me or cure,
So I think I will go there an' see.

56 *The Return*

(ALL ARMS)

Peace is declared, an' I return
  To 'Ackneystadt, but not the same;
Things 'ave transpired which made me learn
  The size and meanin' of the game.
I did no more than others did,
  I don't know where the change began;
I started as a average kid,
  I finished as a thinkin' man.

If England was what England seems,
  An' not the England of our dreams,
But only putty, brass, an' paint,
  'Ow quick we'd drop 'er! But she ain't!

Before my gappin' mouth could speak
 I 'eard it in my comrade's tone;
I saw it on my neighbour's cheek
 Before I felt it flush my own.
An' last it come to me — not pride,
 Nor yet conceit, but on the 'ole
(If such a term may be applied),
 The makin's of a bloomin' soul.

Rivers at night that cluck an' jeer,
 Plains which the moonshine turns to sea,
Mountains that never let you near,
 An' stars to all eternity;
An' the quick-breathin' dark that fills
 The 'ollows of the wilderness,
When the wind worries through the 'ills —
 These may 'ave taught me more or less.

Towns without people, ten times took,
 An' ten times left an' burned at last;
An' starvin' dogs that come to look
 For owners when a column passed;
An' quiet, 'omesick talks between
 Men, met by night, you never knew
Until — 'is face — by shellfire seen —
 Once — an' struck off. They taught me too.

The day's lay-out — the mornin' sun
 Beneath your 'at-brim as you sight;
The dinner-'ush from noon till one,
 An' the full roar that lasts till night;
An' the pore dead that look so old
 An' was so young an hour ago,
An' legs tied down before they're cold —
 These are the things which make you know.

The Settler

Also Time runnin' into years —
    A thousand Places left be'ind —
An' Men from both two 'emispheres
    Discussin' things of every kind;
So much more near than I 'ad known,
    So much more great than I 'ad guessed —
An' me, like all the rest, alone —
    But reachin' out to all the rest!

So 'ath it come to me — not pride,
    Nor yet conceit, but on the 'ole
(If such a term may be applied),
    The makin's of a bloomin' soul.
But now, discharged, I fall away
    To do with little things again. . . .
Gawd, 'oo knows all I cannot say,
    Look after me in Thamesfontein!

If England was what England seems,
    An' not the England of our dreams,
But only putty, brass, an' paint,
    'Ow quick we'd chuck 'er! But she ain't!

57 *The Settler*

Here, where my fresh-turned furrows run,
    And the deep soil glistens red,
I will repair the wrong that was done
    To the living and the dead.
Here, where the senseless bullet fell,
    And the barren shrapnel burst,
I will plant a tree, I will dig a well,
    Against the heat and the thirst.

Here, in a large and a sunlit land,
    Where no wrong bites to the bone,
I will lay my hand in my neighbour's hand,
    And together we will atone
For the set folly and the red breach
    And the black waste of it all,
Giving and taking counsel each
    Over the cattle-kraal.

Here will we join against our foes —
    The hailstroke and the storm,
And the red and rustling cloud that blows
    The locust's mile-deep swarm;
Frost and murrain and floods let loose
    Shall launch us side by side
In the holy wars that have no truce
    'Twixt seed and harvest tide.

Earth, where we rode to slay or be slain,
    Our love shall redeem unto life;
We will gather and lead to her lips again
    The waters of ancient strife,
From the far and the fiercely guarded streams
    And the pools where we lay in wait,
Till the corn cover our evil dreams
    And the young corn our hate.

And when we bring old fights to mind,
    We will not remember the sin —
If there be blood on his head of my kind,
    Or blood on my head of his kin —
For the ungrazed upland, the untilled lea
    Cry, and the fields forlorn:
'The dead must bury their dead, but ye —
    Ye serve an host unborn.'

The Settler

Bless then, our God, the new-yoked plough
    And the good beasts that draw,
And the bread we eat in the sweat of our brow
    According to Thy Law.
After us cometh a multitude –
    Prosper the work of our hands.
That we may feed with our land's food
    The folk of all our lands!

Here, in the waves and the troughs of the plains,
    Where the healing stillness lies,
And the vast, benignant sky restrains
    And the long days make wise –
Bless to our use the rain and the sun
    And the blind seed in its bed,
That we may repair the wrong that was done
    To the living and the dead!

IV Epitaphs of the Great War

(from *The Years Between*, 1919)

58 *'Equality of Sacrifice'*

A. 'I was a "have." ' *B.* 'I was a "have-not." '
(*Together*). 'What hast thou given which I gave not?'

59 *A Servant*

We were together since the War began.
He was my servant — and the better man.

60 *A Son*

My son was killed while laughing at some jest. I would I knew
What it was, and it might serve me in a time when jests are few.

61 An Only Son

I have slain none except my Mother. She
(Blessing her slayer) died of grief for me.

62 Ex-Clerk

Pity not! The Army gave
Freedom to a timid slave:
In which Freedom did he find
Strength of body, will, and mind:
By which strength he came to prove
Mirth, Companionship, and Love:
For which Love to Death he went:
In which Death he lies content.

63 The Wonder

Body and Spirit I surrendered whole
To harsh Instructors — and received a soul . . .
If mortal man could change me through and through
From all I was — what may The God not do?

64 Hindu Sepoy in France

This man in his own country prayed we know not to what Powers
We pray Them to reward him for his bravery in ours.

65 The Beginner

On the first hour of my first day
In the front trench I fell.
(Children in boxes at a play
Stand up to watch it well.)

66 The Favour

Death favoured me from the first, well knowing I could not endure
To wait on him day by day. He quitted my betters and came
Whistling over the fields, and, when he had made all sure,
'Thy line is at end,' he said, 'but at least I have saved its name.'

67 The Refined Man

I was of delicate mind. I stepped aside for my needs,
Disdaining the common office. I was seen from afar and
killed. . . .
How is this matter for mirth? Let each man be judged by his deeds.
I have paid my price to live with myself on the terms that I willed.

68 The Coward

I could not look on Death, which being known,
Men led me to him, blindfold and alone.

151

69 The Sleepy Sentinel

Faithless the watch that I kept: now I have none to keep.
I was slain because I slept: now I am slain I sleep.
Let no man reproach me again, whatever watch is unkept –
I sleep because I am slain. They slew me because I slept.

70 Shock

My name, my speech, my self I had forgot.
My wife and children came – I knew them not.
I died. My Mother followed. At her call
And on her bosom I remembered all.

71 Salonikan Grave

I have watched a thousand days
Push out and crawl into night
Slowly as tortoises.
Now I, too, follow these.
It is fever, and not fight –
Time, not battle – that slays.

72 Native Water-Carrier (M.E.F.)

Prometheus brought down fire to men.
This brought up water.
The Gods are jealous – now, as then,
They gave no quarter.

73 Bombed in London

On land and sea I strove with anxious care
To escape conscription. It was in the air!

74 Batteries out of Ammunition

If any mourn us in the workshop, say
We died because the shift kept holiday.

75 Common Form

If any question why we died,
Tell them, because our fathers lied.

76 Gethsemane

The Garden called Gethsemane
    In Picardy it was,
And there the people came to see
    The English soldiers pass.
We used to pass – we used to pass
    Or halt, as it might be,
And ship our masks in case of gas
    Beyond Gethsemane.

The Garden called Gethsemane,
    It held a pretty lass,

But all the time she talked to me
   I prayed my cup might pass.
The officer sat on the chair,
   The men lay on the grass,
And all the time we halted there
   I prayed my cup might pass —

It didn't pass — it didn't pass —
   It didn't pass from me,
I drank it when we met the gas
   Beyond Gethsemane.

Explanatory Notes

FIRST SERIES, collected in the volumes *Barrack-Room Ballads, and Other Verses* (London, 1892). Twelve of them had appeared in an American edition with some of Kipling's earlier verse at the end of 1890.

1 THE WIDOW AT WINDSOR (first printed in the *Scots Observer* (*SO*) 26 April 1890, as 'Sons of the Widow'). No. 7 of the original twelve. In November 1890 the journal's name was changed to *National Observer*.

There is no warrant for the widespread rumour that Queen Victoria took offence. She did not veto Kipling's appointment as Poet Laureate.

A hairy gold crown. Hairy is a mere emphatic, perhaps a euphemism for bloody. For this, and 'beggar' as a euphemism for 'bugger', see Introduction, p. 19.

The queen's *nick*, her *mark* is the historic crown brand of a broad arrow, ↟. *Lodge o' the Widow* and *tiling* the Lodge are masonic allusions. For *Wings of the Morning* see Psalm 139.

2 TOMMY (*SO* No. 2, 1 March 1890). Thomas Atkins, the traditional name for an English soldier, was selected by Wellington for a specimen signature on an identity card. The original Atkins was a good soldier, killed when under Wellington's first command in 1794.

The *trooper* is a ship chartered to carry soldiers on service overseas. *Goin' large a bit* is misbehaving in the streets.

For *thin red line* see Introduction, p. 21.

3 THE YOUNG BRITISH SOLDIER (*SO* No. 11, 28 June 1890).
An old soldier gives advice to young recruits who will shortly
be drafted to India. The *rag-box* is where he keeps his clean-
ing material. The butt of his Martini rifle is protected by a
steel plate. Cholera was still incurable in 1890, and the super-
stition still prevailed that direct tropical sunshine was deadly.
Fatigue is army slang for extra work at some menial chore. To
crack and *blind* is to use bad language.

Don't call your Martini a . . . bitch. For the Martini rifle,
see Introduction, p. 21. A rifle, like a ship, is always 'she'.
Don't blame her if you can't shoot straight. An old army joke is
the Irish sergeant who said, 'Your rifle is your best friend. More
than that. Treat her like your wife . . . Rub her over every day
with an oily rag.'

When shakin' their bustles. . . . For artillery in action see
Introduction, p. 26. In the frontier campaigns the Pathans
gave no quarter. Your wounded would be killed, perhaps tor-
tured, if left in enemy hands.

4 BELTS (*SO* No. 13, 26 July 1890). This ballad is a rewritten
version of some lines which Kipling printed in his Indian
newspaper in 1888. It is there ascribed to 'Private Mulvaney'
and the name of the regiment is the 18th Royal Irish. The last
of the original series of 'barrack-room ballads'. A high-
spirited scuffle between an English and an Irish regiment,
stationed in Dublin, that grew into a dangerous riot, but with
no hint of any political significance. The Irish speaker uses
some characteristic Dublin expressions, but the conventional
stage-Irish of the Mulvaney stories is not reproduced.

Revelly (*reveillée*) is the bugle call that rouses the troops in
the morning; *Delhi Rebels* and *Threes About* are opprobrious
nicknames for regiments implying, in the first instance, that the
Irish regiment had behaved badly in the Indian Mutiny, in
the second that in some battle the English cavalry had been
left stranded when their horse holders, numbers three in each

Explanatory Notes

section of four men, had run away. The *Freeman's Journal* was the principal Dublin newspaper. A *side-arm* is a bayonet which would have been worn, sheathed, at the belts of the picket sent to restore order.

5 CELLS (*National Observer* (*NO*) 29 November 1890). The latest in date of the first series of ballads, written in a more restrained version of Cockney than the others. It recounts the alcoholic remorse of a drunken soldier confined in the regimental guardhouse, awaiting a summary trial before the colonel at the *Ord'ly room*, his office. He expects as a punishment fourteen days' confinement to barracks (*CB*); some hours of *pack-drill*, that is, monotonous tramping up and down in heavy marching order; forfeiture of pay for the period of CB; and loss of the good-conduct *stripes* on his sleeve.

A *button-stick* is a slotted strip of metal into which the soldier inserts the row of buttons on his tunic so as to polish them without soiling the cloth. Such was the taste in his mouth.

6 ROUTE MARCHIN'. The Grand Trunk Road was the main line of communication from the North-West Frontier to the base camps of the army. Regiments moving up or down marched the 500 miles between Ambala and Cawnpore in about four weeks, pitching camp every evening, striking camp every morning, and resting on Sundays.

Kiko Kissywarsti, don't you hamsher argy jow is pidgin-Hindustani for 'why don't you make way?' To *sling the bat* is to talk a jargon of pidgin-English and pidgin-Hindustani. The *rookies* are the new recruits; the women with children are wives married 'on the strength' (see note 3). *Injia's coral strand* is a reminiscence of the missionary hymn, 'From Greenland's icy mountains'.

7 SCREW-GUNS (*SO* No. 12, 12 July 1890). For screw-guns, see Introduction, p. 27.

The *Naga*, the *Looshai* and the *Afreedee* (or Afridi) are

157

tribes of the North-West Frontier; 2,000 yards was the effective range of the screw-guns; *drag-ropes* might be used by teams of soldiers to replace or supplement the mules; *long-eared old darlin's* were the mules which deserved a better reputation than they usually got. *'Tss, 'Tss* is the traditional noise made by men grooming horses or mules, to blow the dust out of their mouths.

8 OONTS (*SO* No. 4, 22 March 1890). The subtitle is *Northern India Transport Train. Oont,* properly pronounced with a vowel sound as in 'bull', is the Hindustani word for camel. Until the mechanical age all armies used camel transport when fighting in desert country. Under suitable conditions camels are valuable beyond price, but in the wrong climate or landscape they are stubbornly uncooperative. The speaker of this ballad is a soldier who dislikes camels, mispronouncing their name to rhyme with 'grunt'. He speaks an unusually illiterate Cockney.

9 THE WIDOW'S PARTY (*NO*, 22 November 1890). This question-and-answer ballad expresses the half-formed political opinions of an illiterate Tommy more simply than No. 1, 'The Widow at Windsor'.

Gosport Hard is the dock at Portsmouth from which the troopships sailed. Notice the emphatic adjective, *bleedin'*, another euphemism for bloody. The *bight of a canvas trough* is an ambulance stretcher.

10 GENTLEMEN-RANKERS. In India, the land of caste, British class distinctions hardened, so that army officers, who were 'gentlemen', formed a high caste of their own, while the rank and file, drawn from the working class, were very low caste indeed. Gentlemen-rankers were upper-class Britons who, for some reason, had dropped out and enlisted as private soldiers. Slightly suspect, they were unpopular with both sides. Very rarely, a gentleman-ranker succeeded in climbing back to the officer class by sheer merit, as did Kipling's schoolfriend,

Explanatory Notes

Brigadier-General F. M. G. Cunliffe, CB (1861–1955), who is mentioned in *The Jungle Book*, who enlisted as a trooper in the 9th Lancers, and ended as a general in the First World War.

For the *Curse of Reuben* see *Genesis*, 29–35 *passim*.

In later editions 'Yea' in the fifth line was altered to 'Yes', an improvement that I have adopted.

11 'SNARLEYOW' (*NO*, 29 November 1890). The odd name is taken from a novel by Captain J. Marryat (1837). We are not told till line 14 that here it is the name of a horse. For artillery procedure, see Introduction, p. 26.

If an infantryman falls down, nobody cares; if a cavalry horse falls, someone will get the rough side of the colonel's tongue; but with the guns, if a leading horse falls while the wheel-horses are being flogged on, the bombardier indeed loses heart because he knows that four horses and 2 tons of ammunition in the limber are coming over him, as they came over the driver's brother.

This is not a contemporary story but an old soldier's reminiscence of the Sikh Wars, forty years back. It is based on an incident in the battle of Ferozeshah, 21 December 1845, described in Sergeant N. W. Bancroft's history of the Bengal Horse Artillery, *From Recruit to Staff Sergeant* (Calcutta, 1885), when the guns still fired *tricky, trundlin' roundshot* which could be seen coming.

12 FORD O' KABUL RIVER (*NO*, 22 November 1890). Based on an incident in the Second Afghan War. During the advance to Kabul, on 31 March 1879, the 10th Hussars made an attempt, by night, to ford the Kabul river, a mountain torrent that flows through the Khyber Pass. The stream rose in flood, drowning an officer and forty-six troopers. The American soldiers' song, 'Tramp, tramp, tramp, the boys are marching', echoes through the refrain.

Strictly speaking, cavalry regiments do not blow bugles but

The Complete Barrack-Room Ballads

trumpets. In some editions, Kipling corrected the second line to 'Blow the trumpet . . .'. Accuracy prevailed over euphony.

13 GUNGA DIN (*SO* No. 9, 7 June 1890). Hackneyed by quotation but a favourite with the soldiers as late as World War I. Based upon the story of Juma, water-carrier to the Frontier Force regiment of The Guides at the siege of Delhi, July 1857. He was selected by his comrades as the bravest man in the regiment (G. F. Younghusband, *Story of the Guides*, pp. 53–4). Hindustani words: *bhisti*, water-carrier; *hitherao panee lao*, bring water quickly; *Harry By . . . juldee*, brother, be quick; *I'll marrow you*, I'll beat you; *mussick*, water skin-bag, *dooli*, ambulance wagon.

14 'FUZZY-WUZZY' (*SO* No. 3, 15 March 1890). Subtitled *Sudan Expeditionary Force*. The Sudanese tribes were formidable adversaries at close quarters in rough ground. *It wasn't 'ardly fair* to slosh them with Martinis at long range. The Beggara tribe of the western Sudan once achieved what Napoleon's armies had never done, by breaking into a square of 1,500 British infantry at Abu Klea, 24 December 1884. It needed confused hand-to-hand fighting before the intruders were killed and the square reformed. The nickname *Fuzzy-Wuzzy* more properly refers to the Hadendowa tribe of the eastern Sudan, who wore their long hair frizzed out. They repeatedly fought the British near Suakin as described in this ballad, and often had the best of it.

The speaker of this ballad has a rich picturesque vocabulary, but all his words may be found in the dictionary. *Paythans* (more properly Pathans) are the tribes of the North-West Frontier. A Zulu *impi* (regiment) almost wiped out the British 24th Regiment at Isandlhwana, 22 January 1879.

15 LOOT (*SO* No. 5, 29 March 1890). Kipling, like Shakespeare, had a soft spot for a gaudy rogue. The speaker in this ballad is

Explanatory Notes

in direct line of descent from 'Ancient Pistol' and his morals are almost as outrageous (see *Henry V*, Act IV, Scene 4). You are not obliged to believe a word he says. It is a joke, though some may think a joke in bad taste.

Clobber means clothes.

16 DANNY DEEVER (*SO* No. 1, 22 February 1890). A question-and-answer ballad, in traditional English form, the first of the *Barrack-Room Ballads* to be published under this serial title, and over Kipling's name. It received an ovation from the sophisticated readers of the *Scots Observer*. Both Yeats and Eliot in later years selected it for special commendation, while expressing their inability to place it in contemporary literature, not knowing that this was the genuine folklore of the London streets. Its structure is based on a crude and ribald song, called in polite society 'Barnacle Bill the Sailor', which presents the same alternation of rhythm and tone between question and answer. But the deeper harmonies and the changes of key, especially in the last verse, are different indeed. The work of a master of language. Note the change from slow to quick time.

Several claims have been made by old soldiers to have known the original Danny Deever, but none are convincing. Though Kipling, as a press reporter, attended several murder trials in the civil courts, there is no evidence that he was concerned with a military execution. Public executions were discontinued in England in 1868, but were carried out in India a few years longer. The graphic description of the effect upon the spectators is derived largely from G. R. Gleig's *The Subaltern*, a reminiscence of the Peninsular War in 1813, published thirty years before Kipling was born. Danny Deever was publicly degraded before execution, by cutting off his regimental buttons and tearing off his conduct stripes.

17 TROOPIN' (*SO* No. 8, 17 May 1890). Every September, when the hot weather ended, drafts of new recruits were shipped out

to India to be acclimatized during the cool weather. Accordingly, men who had served their six years were shipped home to England where they would arrive in *Injian cotton kit* in time for the winter. A fleet of transports, including the *Jumna* and the *Malabar*, was chartered to exchange old for new soldiers between Portsmouth and Bombay. The six-year men returned to civil life as reservists, with a retaining fee of 4d. a day, a trifling sum even in those days.

18 SOLDIER, SOLDIER (*SO* No. 6, 12 April 1890). Following immediately upon No. 8, 'Oonts', and No. 15, 'Loot', this ballad opened a new field with its delicacy and simplicity. Both voices speak with restraint and compassion. Some readers may be reminded of A. E. Housman, but Kipling was no imitator here. This ballad was published six years before *A Shropshire Lad*.

Note that the dead soldier wore *rifle-green*. The rifle regiments were raised during the American wars for forest fighting and were dressed in green for protective coloration. They were trained to act independently as scouts and sharp-shooters: *I seed 'im runnin' by when the shots begun to fly.*

19 MANDALAY (*SO* No. 10, 21 June 1890). Perhaps the favourite among the 'barrack-room ballads', written to a popular waltz tune, set to music as a tenor song, and long since passed into folklore. 'Mandalay' was adopted by the Americans and rewritten for 'Panama'. Recently it has been copied by Bertolt Brecht.

Kipling paid only one visit to Burma, in March 1889, when his ship called at Rangoon and Moulmein. The scene-painting of this song, he says (*Something of Myself*, p. 221), is 'a sort of mix-up . . . of the singer's memories against a background of the Bay of Bengal as seen at dawn from a troopship'. The subject is the nostalgia that the returned soldier in London feels for the warm and sensuous East.

Explanatory Notes

The conquest of Upper Burma, in 1885, had involved a river campaign depending on the Irrawaddy flotilla which plied from Rangoon to Mandalay. There was little fighting and the people of Lower Burma were friendly to the British soldiers.

The pretext for the British invasion of the north was disorder following the death of King Theebaw, whose queen was Supi-yaw-lat; *hathis* are elephants.

For a discussion of the language of this ballad, see Introduction, p. 17.

20 SHILLIN' A DAY. Written to the tune of the famous old Cockney song, 'Vilikins and his Dinah', in a restrained Irish brogue. *Birr* is in Ireland, *Leeds* in northern England, *Hong-Kong* in China, and the other placenames in northern India. A *Ghazi* is a Moslem devotee, somewhat like a Japanese *Kamikaze*.

O'Kelly must go *commissairin'*. The uniformed Royal Corps of Commissionaires were reliable old soldiers recruited to take charge of valuables or carry confidential messages.

SECOND SERIES, mostly written in Vermont, 1893–5. Collected, except for Nos. 31 and 36, in *The Seven Seas*, published by Methuen, London, October 1896.

21 'BACK TO THE ARMY AGAIN' (*Pall Mall Magazine*, August 1894). A reservist, unemployed in London, re-enlists under a false name. The drill sergeant and the sergeant-tailor are well aware that he is an old soldier, but wink at it. An *ulster* is a tweed overcoat; a *billycock* hat is now called a bowler; *slops* are his new recruit's uniform. The speaker's asides to the sergeant mention words of command with which he shows himself acquainted.

22 'BIRDS OF PREY' MARCH (*Pall Mall Gazette*, 30 May 1895). Ribald choruses by soldiers embarking in the rain for

some colonial war. The refrain may be sung to the tune of Albert Chevalier's 'Knocked 'em in the Old Kent Road'. In the third verse, *slingers* are 'hard tack', ship's biscuits soaked in tea. In the fourth, the ironic reference is to the War Office, which then occupied the building in Whitehall where the mounted sentries stand.

23 THE 'EATHEN (*McClure's Magazine*, September 1896, but written a year earlier: cf. No. 3, 'The Young British Soldier'). The title is borrowed from a missionary hymn and is applied to illiterates who do not appreciate the national tradition. It is not addressed to the young recruits but is an old soldier's reminiscence of his own observations. The moral comes at the end: *The backbone of the Army is the non-commissioned man.*

Abby-nay, kul, hazar-ho are pidgin-Hindustani words for not now, tomorrow, wait a bit.

In the fifth verse, notice *'E learns to drop the 'bloodies'*, that is to use the soldiers' meaningless vogue word. In the sixth and seventh verses the recruit is appointed lance-corporal, an acting rank, on trial for promotion, with responsibility but no extra pay. *Colour-Sergeant* was the highest rank a private soldier could hope to reach. Originally he carried the regimental 'colour'; he is the guardian of *esprit de corps* – has *the Core at 'eart.* *An' now the hugly bullets come peckin'*, a description of coming under fire comparable only with that in the *Chartreuse de Parme*.

24 'THE MEN THAT FOUGHT AT MINDEN'. An old soldier instructs recruits in the regimental tradition in his own way. At the battle of Minden in Germany, 1 August 1759, an allied army under Prince Ferdinand of Brunswick defeated the French, the honours of the day going to a brigade of British infantry. They fought in a rose garden and for 200 years went on parade every 1 August wearing roses in their caps.

One of the Minden regiments was the 5th (Northumberland Fusiliers), well known to Kipling at Lahore in 1885–7. The stocks beneath their chins, and the exaggerated number of *buttons up an' down* are borrowed from Sergeant Bancroft (see note 12). To *club* a parade is to bungle the drill movements and get into a disorderly crowd; *musketoons* and *halberds* were eighteenth-century weapons; a *Johnny Raw* is a recruit.

25 BILL 'AWKINS (*Pall Mall Gazette*, 2 May 1895). A piece of light verse. Note that the second speaker has a faint Irish brogue.

26 THE SHUT-EYE SENTRY (*Pearson's Magazine*, November 1896: called *The Four Guardsmen* in some editions). In barracks, a subaltern is appointed orderly officer for the day and remains constantly on duty to deal with domestic routine and with any emergencies that may arise when the others are off duty. One of his tasks is to inspect the sentries and *turn out the Guard* at irregular intervals. He is assisted by an orderly sergeant, an orderly corporal and several orderly men. In this case it is the sentry who inspects the orderly officer, and decides to turn a blind eye. *Hokee-mut* is Hindustani for drunk; visiting *Rounds* is the name for inspection of the guard; the *affidavit* is the witness's oath at a court-martial, if it had come to that; *'elp him for 'is mother* is a masonic allusion.

27 THE SERGEANT'S WEDDIN' (*McClure's Magazine*, September 1896). A rare example of a Kipling ballad that was heavily revised by the author. For example, lines 25–8 originally ran

> 'E 'as scores agin us,
> Tick for more than beer,
> Clean against the orders,
> That is why we're here.

and the refrain baldly stated 'An' a rogue is married to a 'ore'. The second verse implies that as canteen sergeant he cheated the men by selling short measure of beer and used his profits to buy a *buggy*, that is, a light, two-horse van. But for his wedding, the sergeant hired a *lando* (landau), that is, a fashionable carriage, and borrowed a pair of grey horses from friends in the artillery.

28 THE MOTHER-LODGE (*Pall Mall Gazette*, 2 May 1895). Kipling wrote this piece in a single day, 29 October 1894, when Conan Doyle was a guest in his house. It is his tribute to free-masonry, the only society in India that transcended race, caste and rank. He had become a freemason at Lahore in 1885. *Level, Square, Junior Deacon, Landmarks,* etc, are allusions to masonic ritual. *Trichies* are Trichinopoly cigars; the *hog-darn* is the lighter; the *khansamah* is the butler; the *bottle-khana* is the pantry.

29 SAPPERS (*Pall Mall Gazette*, 25 April 1895). Perhaps not spoken by a Royal Engineer, but by a soldier of the line making quiet fun of the 'Sappers' (formerly called 'The Royal Corps of Sappers and Miners') who gave themselves airs as being technicians as well as good soldiers. They were regarded with ironical respect for their serious attitude to life, 'mad, married or methodist'. The Sapper speaks a more correct English than the common Tommy, and is well read, at least in the Bible.

30 'SOLDIER AND SAILOR TOO' (*Pearson's Magazine*, April 1896). Spoken by a soldier looking over the side of a troopship in the Suez Canal (*spittin' into the Ditch aboard o' the Crocodile*) and watching a marine at work. He is puzzled by the marine's anomalous position, which he describes in misused learned words (*Harumfrodite* for hermaphrodite, *cosmopolouse* for cos-mopolite, *procrastitute* for procrastinate, and *chrysanthemum* (?)). He calls the marines by the nineteenth-century nickname, *Jollies,* which has fallen out of use; his picturesque turns of phrase speak for themselves.

Since the seventeenth century the Royal Navy has carried detachments of soldiers on the larger ships for specifically military tasks, such as landing parties, or using 'small-arms'. When not otherwise occupied, they may be called on to assist the sailors. The 'Red Marines' were trained as light infantry, the 'Blue Marines' as artillery.

The third verse refers to rivalry between marines and ordinary soldiers, the fourth alludes to some minor mutinies, mere strikes against bad conditions, in the old army, from which the speaker moves to 'finishing in style'. First to the heroic story of the *Birkenhead* shipwreck, off the South African coast in 1852, when the soldiers stood to arms on the quarterdeck and went down with the ship in order to hold her on an even keel while the women and children were saved; secondly to the loss of the battleship *Victoria*, after a collision during manœuvres in the Mediterranean, 22 June 1893. The marines attempted to repeat the 'Birkenhead drill'. When the admiral gave the order to abandon ship, all being lost, the marines first went below in a vain attempt to close the watertight doors. Both the officers and 99 out of 120 men were drowned. (*The Times*, 28 June 1893.)

31 'BOBS' (the history of this piece is obscure. Written and printed in 1893, it was suppressed, presumably because Lord Roberts didn't like it. Not included in a 'collected' edition before his death in 1914).

For the career of Lord Roberts ('Bobs') see Introduction, p. 22. *Bahadur* is a Hindustani title of honour for a high commander; *Kandaharder* is doggerel for the title, Lords Roberts of Kandahar; '*Dook of Aggy Chel*', a Cockney-Hindustani joke for Duke of Go-ahead; verse three refers to his eye for military detail, verse four to his campaign against drunkenness; verse five to his battle experience. *Pocket-Wellin'ton an' arder* means 'a little man, but a Wellington-and-a-half'.

32 THE JACKET (*McClure's Magazine*, September 1896). For artillery procedure, see Introduction, p. 26, and 'Snarleyow', note 12.

This episode has been associated with Captain J. Dalbiac, a well-known practical joker who was selected for the senior corps, the Royal Horse Artillery, when serving in the Egyptian

War of 1882, and celebrated his assumption of the more decorative 'jacket' of the horse-gunners with a round of drinks for his men, during which they got involved in a skirmish. He had brought up to the battery position three dozen bottles of beer (*Bass*) in a limber which should have carried thirty-six *crackers*, case-shot and shrapnel.

The *Arabites* were the followers of Arābi Pasha, the Egyptian nationalist leader. The British had intervened, unwisely perhaps, on the side of the legitimate government. Instead of bombarding a *sand redoubt*, an entrenchment in the desert, the gunners charged it, wheeling and opening fire when they reached the *glassy* (*glacis*), the cleared slope in front of the trench.

Dalbiac was killed in the South African War in 1900.

33 THAT DAY (*Pall Mall Gazette*, 25 April 1895). A reminiscence of defeat, probably collected by Kipling when he visited the sergeants' mess of the 66th (Royal Berkshire) Regiment at Bermuda in March 1894. The tale tells of an incident in the Battle of Maiwand, 27 July 1880, when a brigade of British and Indian troops were defeated by Afghan regulars, led by a force of *ghazis* (religious devotees). One wing of the regiment, with the colonel, fought and died to the last man; the other wing made a scrambling retreat to Kandahar. It was on this occasion that Roberts saved the situation by marching 300 miles across the mountains to their relief.

Sove-ki-poo is the soldier's rendering of *sauve-qui-peut*.

34 CHOLERA CAMP (*McClure's Magazine*, October 1896). The cause of cholera was imperfectly known and half its victims died when Kipling was in India. Even in England there had been uncontrollable epidemics as recently as 1866. If a regiment took cholera, the only remedy was to move away from the infected area.

Nullahs are water-courses; *Lances actin' Sergeants* are lance-corporals (see note 23); *Ta-ra-ra-Boom-der-ay*, a famous music-hall ditty sung by Lottie Collins; *padre*, an army chaplain, Catholic or Protestant.

The last verse includes the drill movements for lowering tents when striking camp.

35 'FOLLOW ME 'OME' (*Pall Mall Magazine*, June 1894). A soldier sitting in the canteen meditates on a dead comrade as he hears the drum and fife band assembling for the funeral. Technically, this ballad is worth study. The language is simple and the vocabulary, though limited, is indeed adequate. (See Introduction, p. 17.)

The irregular stanza, *Take 'im away* . . . is composed to the tune of Handel's 'Dead March'. The final stanza refers to the three volleys traditionally fired over a soldier's grave by thirteen of his comrades.

For *passin' the love o' women*, see *II Samuel*, 1.26.

36 'MY GIRL, SHE GIVE ME THE GO ONST' (Actually the earliest of the ballads, but out of series. It is sung by Private Ortheris in the story, 'The Courting of Dinah Shadd', printed in *Macmillan's Magazine*, December 1889 and collected in the volume, *Life's Handicap*, 1891).

Kipling's early stories contain many snatches of soldiers' song. This is the only one that seems to me to qualify as a barrack-room ballad.

A *dah* is a short sword carried by a Burman. A *full C.B.* is a sentence of confinement to barracks. See 'Cells' (No. 5).

37 THE LADIES (*Pall Mall Gazette*, 2 May 1895). The last quatrain became one of Kipling's most familiar quotations. *Prome* is in Burma; a *jemadar-sais* is a head groom; *'Oogli* (Hooghly) is a suburb of Calcutta named after the river; *Actin' in charge o' Bazar*, acting as sergeant in charge of the regimental store and canteen; *Neemuch* (Nimach) is in Rajasthan, India; *Mhow* is in Central India; *bolee* is the gypsy language; *Meerut* is near Delhi.

38 'MARY, PITY WOMEN!' (*Pall Mall Magazine*, February 1894). Somewhat of a surprise after the other ballads. In the manner of Browning's *Dramatic Lyrics*. Note the solidity, the reality, of the silent listener. The interested reader should notice the affinity with 'Record of Badalia Herodsfoot' (see Introduction, p. 14). This is one of the ballads that influenced Bertolt Brecht.

39 FOR TO ADMIRE (*Pall Mall Gazette*, February 1894). A soldier who has completed his service returns to England in a troopship, manned by *lascars*, the hereditary caste of sailors from western India. His call as watchman from the crows-nest is *Hum deckty hai*, 'I'm looking out'. *Sat in Clink without my boots*, see 'Cells' (note 5). If prisoners were violent, their boots were removed to prevent kicking.

The description of the rock of Aden is apt.

THIRD SERIES (Boer War Ballads) written between 1899 and 1903, and 'collected' in the volume *The Five Nations* as 'Service Songs' (Methuen, 1903), excepting No. 40.

40 THE ABSENT-MINDED BEGGAR (printed in the *Daily Mail* on 31 October 1899, a few days after the outbreak of war; not 'collected' until the Bombay edition, 1914).

This is not a recruiting song, as it is often described, but an appeal for funds to help the soldiers' families while *the man that earns the wage is ordered out*. By giving general permission to circulate it, Kipling raised over £250,000 for family aid. It was set to a tune by Elgar and sung 'on the Halls'. It was merely an occasional piece and Kipling afterwards suppressed it for some years.

In army slang an absent-minded beggar (bugger) is a well-meaning soldier who is careless and forgetful. The strength of this phrase will be felt in lines 21–4. Kipling sees no merit in abusing Paul Kruger, the Transvaal president. *Wiping*

Explanatory Notes

something off a slate is reversing the decision of the First Boer War, 1880, when the Boers had the best of it. The mention of 50,000 horse and foot astonished the civilians who then first learned they were in for a large-scale war. It came to many more than that. *Table Bay* is the harbour of Cape Town.

This ballad is not rendered in broad Cockney but in decent middle-class London vernacular.

It contains echoes of the charming old soldiers' song that the original Thomas Atkins had once sung, 'The Girl I Left Behind Me'.

41 STELLENBOSH (More properly spelled in the Afrikaans form 'Stellenbosch'). In every army, in every war, a problem is the general who has arrived at the summit too late, after a distinguished career – how to replace him courteously by a younger, more flexible commander. In the Boer War the British base camp was at Stellenbosch, near Cape Town. Generals eased out of their commands were relegated to administrative tasks at the base. The verb, 'to stellenbosch', survived as a term for polite supersession.

Boojers are *burghers*, Dutch for 'citizens' of the republic. The name 'Afrikaner' for 'Boer' was not yet in use; the *stoep*, pronounced 'stoop', is the terrace; the *drift* is the ford of the river, words in common use in South Africa; the *'elios* are heliographs, light signals used before the days of radio; KCB and DSO are decorations he and his staff hoped to get; *sugared about*, a euphemism for buggered about.

42 TWO KOPJES. Pronounced 'copies', the Afrikaans name for flat-topped rocky hills, a common feature of the landscape, easily converted into fortresses. A *visit, unarmed, to the Rand* is a column of prisoners on their way to Waterval. See note 51. *Cornelius* and *Piet* are soldiers' nicknames for the Boers.

43 THE INSTRUCTOR (with the subtitle, *Corporals*). This piece is in correct ballad-form with five-line stanzas. Though rendered in full Cockney pronunciation, it is put in the mouth

of a thoughtful man with a rich vocabulary and a sense of language; it is full of allusive phrases. The 'instructors' are the bullets passing overhead as men lie hidden in the grass, able to move only by a *belly-crawl*.

Old Nickel Neck is a double or triple pun. The bullets used by both armies were of soft lead enclosed in a collar of hard nickel which kept shape in the rifle grooves, these ensuring accurate shooting; the first of the early British defeats had been at Nicholson's Nek near Ladysmith, where many soldiers first met that grim instructor, death. *Fitzy van Spitz* is a nonsense word for Boer bullets spluttering as they break up among the rocks. The *peevish voice* is the whine of a ricochet; the *'oary mushroom 'ead* is the soft grey lead which mushrooms out of the nickel collar and enlarges the wound.

The ballad contains an early reference to the cinematograph.

44 BOOTS (with the subtitle *Infantry Columns of the Earlier War*). There is evidence that Kipling had made a draft of this fifteen years earlier, when watching manoeuvres in India. It may be sung to the tune of 'John Brown's Body'.

45 THE MARRIED MAN (subtitle *Reservist of the Line*). cf. No. 40, 'The Absent-Minded Beggar'.

46 UBIQUE. The motto of the Royal Artillery (see Introduction, p. 26) is *Ubique* (Latin for 'everywhere') implying that they do not win particular battle honours because they are present at every battle.

The second verse suggests artillery duels with the Boers' Krupp guns; the third verse moves from long-range, *Blue Fuse* with the gun dug in and tilted upwards, to short-range with the gunners and their horses under rifle fire, as at Colenso in 1899. The fourth treats of drives as easy as a London busride, and the fifth of river crossings. The *khaki muzzles* are gun muzzles. *Shellin' all outdoors* means an aim confused by mirages. The sixth verse refers to the last phase of the war when mounted infantry were in greater demand than artillery (see 'M. I.', note 48). The seventh verse comes back to the final dependence of infantry (*the linesman*) upon artillery. *De Wet* was the famous guerrilla leader who outwitted many British columns. (See next note.)

47 COLUMNS (subtitle *Mobile Columns of the Later War*). Kitchener's success in the guerrilla war was won by protecting the pacified districts with guarded fences of barbed wire and by hunting the Boer commandos with mobile columns under his own direction, as many as sixty in the field together at one time. A typical column might consist of one battalion of infantry (600 men), one section of artillery (two 15-pounder field guns) and a *pompom*, an experimental light gun that fired six 1-pound shells in rapid succession.

48 M. I. (subtitle, *Mounted Infantry of the Line: Windsor Magazine*, October 1901). A footnote in the early editions said 'fill in the number of the M. I. Regiment "to taste".'

For the use of mounted infantry, see Introduction, p. 26.

The M. I. were known as *Ikonas*, 'ikona' being Afrikaans slang for ready, probably of Bantu origin, O.K., make-do.

Their one complaint was that the Australian volunteers were paid 5s. a day for the same duty as the British Tommies at 1s. a day.

49 LICHTENBERG (subtitle, *New South Wales Contingent*). Kipling had spent only a few days in Australia. His knowledge of Australians was of their volunteers in the Boer War. It is credibly reported that he overheard an Australian saying 'I smelt wattle at Lichtenberg, ridin' in, in the rain', and so wrote the ballad. The wattle, a variety of mimosa, is the national flower of Australia, and is common as a garden shrub in South Africa. Lichtenberg in the western Transvaal was the scene of several minor actions during Roberts's advance. (See Introduction, p. 25.)

50 THE PARTING OF THE COLUMNS. The title of the book, *The Five Nations*, is explained by this piece. The Boer War had made the British Commonwealth a reality.

Kruger cut and run: Kruger went into exile in Holland after Roberts's victories. *Bloemingtyphoidtein* is Bloemfontein, pronounced 'Bloom-f'n-tain', capital of the Orange Free State, where Roberts's army was decimated by an epidemic of typhoid. *Calgary* is in western, *Quebec* and *Montreal* in eastern Canada; *Dawson* is in northern Canada, *Galle* in Ceylon; *Darwin* in northern and *Sydney* in southern Australia; *Wellington* in northern and *Timaru* (pronounced 'Timmer-roo') in southern New Zealand. The kea, the wild green New Zealand parrot, was believed, perhaps unjustly, to attack lambs.

51 HALF-BALLAD OF WATERVAL. The verse form is correctly described as a 'half-ballad'.

Some hundreds of British prisoners of war, taken in the early Boer victories, were confined at Waterval near Pretoria until they were released by Lord Roberts's advance. When Boer prisoners became numerous in the later war, they were interned in Ceylon or St Helena.

52 BRIDGE-GUARD IN THE KARROO (*The Times*, 5 June 1901). An extract, printed below this title, from the *District Orders, Lines of Communications* runs: '. . . and will supply details to guard the Blood River Bridge'. The main railway from Cape Town to Johannesburg crosses the desolate plateau known as the Karroo. Blood River Station is about 200 miles up the line.

53 'WILFUL-MISSING'. A 'dropout's' story.
aasvogel, the vulture; the *Low Bush-veldt* is the coastal plain; *Domino* is the word with which you declare the game finished.

54 PIET (subtitle, *Regular of the Line*). The regular soldier must respect and might nourish a sort of affection for his opponent, to whom he gave the nickname *Piet*. The Boers, a citizen

army, having no uniforms, fought in their working clothes. As the war progressed they had no hesitation in wearing captured British uniforms and boots, stripping their prisoners and releasing them half-naked. Though contrary to the 'laws of war', this conduct was condoned by the British authorities.

The *stony kop* is a hill fortress; *biltong* is dried meat; *awful Dop* is Cape brandy; a *Mauser* is a German type of rifle; *From Plewman's to Marabastad*, *From Ookiep to De Aar* is from south to north, from west to east. The last stanza refers to the contribution by the British taxpayer to the cost of reconstruction, a new precedent in the history of conquest.

55 CHANT-PAGAN (*Windsor Magazine*, October 1901). (Subtitle, *English Irregular: '99–'02*.)

The *Ma'ollisberg* (Magaliesberg) *Range*, west of Johannesburg, was a stronghold of the guerrilla leader, de la Rey.

Dundee was the scene of the first fighting in northern Natal; *Vereeniging*, near Pretoria, was the scene of the Boer surrender. *Di'mond 'ill* was Roberts's defeat of Botha; *Pieters, Springs, Belfast*, other actions in the Transvaal.

56 THE RETURN (subtitle, *All Arms*).

'Ackneystadt, Thamesfontein: comical names in Afrikaans for the East End, and for London in general.

57 THE SETTLER (*The Times*, 23 February 1903). Kipling's valediction, put in the mouth of a literate soldier, a year after the end of the war.

General Smuts, after fighting to the bitter end, also appealed for a generous peace. 'History', he said, 'writes the word "Reconciliation" over all her quarrels.' Alas, not so.

FOURTH SERIES. A series of thirty-five *Epitaphs of the War*, written by Kipling in 1917–18 was published in his volume of verse, *The Years Between*, in 1919. Eighteen of them, in most of which soldiers account for their own deaths, are reproduced here.

He wrote much other verse about the war, notably about sailors, but the only other piece that comes within my definition of a barrack-room ballad is No. 76, 'Gethsemane', which also first appeared in *The Years Between*.

Nos. 58–75: For a general note on the epitaphs, see Introduction, p. 12. No. 67 originally read, 'I went aside'. I have adopted the reading 'stepped aside' from later editions.

76 GETHSEMANE. Some readers have found this piece obscure. Kipling writing to a friend said that it referred 'to the horror that overtakes a man when he first ships his gas-mask. What makes war most poignant is the presence of women with whom he can talk and make love, only an hour or so behind the line.'

Note the assonance, or near-rhyme of *was, lass, grass, pass, gas*. This is not a Cockney ballad and the speaker may be using a dialect in which these syllables have a common value. Or Kipling may be making a deliberate experiment in partial rhymes as did the young war poet, Wilfrid Owen, at the same date.